SIGRID SCHACHT

HELGE VANGMARK

Russian-English
Basic Dictionary

63816

John Murray
50 Albemarle Street
London, England

EMC Corporation
180 East Sixth Street
St. Paul, Minnesota, USA

Cover design: IB JØRGENSEN

John Murray ISBN 07195 2881 X
EMC Corporation ISBN 0-88436-063-6

ANDELSBOGTRYKKERIET I ODENSE

MCMLXXIII

Preface

The Russian-English Basic Dictionary contains 2,400 entries listed alphabetically. A, B or C by an entry indicates the frequency range into which words fall: A – 1000 words; B – 1800 words; C – 2400 words. Each entry includes the necessary grammatical information and idioms.

The Dictionary is designed to cover most of Russian vocabulary in ordinary use and aid those wishing to read Russian texts. It also offers complete coverage of the words and idioms used in the series of Russian Easy Readers, whose controlled vocabularies are based on it.

The Dictionary was compiled in the following way:

An initial listing was based on material in Josselson, *The Russian Word Count*, 1953, and Steinfeldt, *Russian Word Count*, 1961, which was repeatedly filtered.

The statistical findings of these two writers are based on counts of word forms, to the effect that e.g. imperfective and perfective verbs, attributive and predicative forms of adjectives, etc., are counted separately. In the Russian-English Basic Dictionary such forms were added to form integers, in the first place to make the Dictionary more handy; secondly, to avoid leaving out words whose absence might create serious obstacles to the composition of readable books; and, thirdly, to avoid an incomplete, even unintelligible, representation of what are accepted as semantic unities by readers whose mother tongue is structured differently from the Russian.

The reliability of the material was checked by comparing it with the following fundamental vocabularies, allegedly based on frequency counts, although no sources are stated:

Anpilogova   *Essential Russian-English Dictionary*, undated.
Waddington   *A Basic Russian-English Vocabulary*, 1962.
Vogt   *Grund- und Aufbauwortschatz Russisch*, 1967.

In addition, a large quantity of mimeographed material from the

State University of Moscow and the Lumumba University has been used.

As the Dictionary was planned as the basis of fictional texts the material was carefully compared with the glossaries of a number (15) of adapted Russian texts, mainly from the series of *Russian Readers for Beginners* and *Easy Russian* (both published in Moscow).

To make sure that the Dictionary covers a sufficient amount of everyday concepts as well as words and phrases of spoken Russian used in fiction the material was compared with:

N. P. Vakar   *A Word Count of Spoken Russian*, 1966.

S. Khavronina   *Russian As We Speak It*, undated.

G. Bogatova   *Practical Russian*, undated.

2380 slov naibolee upotrebitel'nykh v russkoi razgovornoi rechi, 1968 (Universitet druzhby narodov).

N. F. Potapova   *The Penguin Russian Course*, 1961.

Arakin/Samoilova   *My First/Second/Third Russian Book*, 1966.

Filatova/Wahlström   *Slova za slovom*, 1960.

Menos & Volos   *Méthode audio-visuelle de russe* (Didier), 1964.

W. Steinbrecht   *Russisch heute*, 1969.

The principles of word selection were discussed with Professor H. Spang-Hanssen, Ph.D. (whose doctoral dissertation: *Probability and Structural Classification in Word Count* was particularly useful).

Pursuing the line of thought that courses like those mentioned above are of importance to the selection of vocabulary, the authors have included the basic and most frequently used rules for Russian word-formation. Consequently, words that may be formed from these rules have been omitted. The list can be found at the beginning of the book and should be studied before the book is used. In this way a larger number of words than those actually included in the Dictionary can be understood.

It is in the nature of language that hard and fast rules cannot be followed meticulously for the selection of words (see the preface to Waddington's work). This is especially true when fixing the range of meaning of words and dealing with the use of high-fre-

4

quency idioms containing low-frequency words, which are often subject to changes of meaning. In numerous cases Ozhegov, *Slovar' russkogo yazyka* (Moscow, 1963) and *Slovar' sovremennogo russkogo literaturnogo* yazyka 1–17 (Akademiya nauk SSSR, Moscow-Leningrad, 1950–65) have served as guides. Many articles in *Russkii yazyk za rubezom* have also been helpful, the latter particularly in giving suggestions for word-lists.

The authors thank Professor Hans Chr. Sørensen, Ph.D., for his interest in their work, and special thanks are due to Mr. Helge Poulsen, Chief Inspector of Secondary Schools, for critical examination of the manuscript.

Sigrid Schacht   *Helge Vangmark*

Notes for users of the Dictionary:

While the range of a dictionary containing only 2,400 main entries is likely to be limited, many words not included can be easily understood by working out meanings from their stems. Knowledge of elementary rules for the formation of Russian words, such as the permutation of consonants mentioned below, is also a very useful means of solving problems of translation.

1) **не-.** Most Russian adjectives and participles may be prefixed with не-, which imparts a negative meaning to them (such as "in-", "un-", or "not"), e. g. неизвéстный (unknown, not known), нетрýдный (not difficult, easy, simple).

2) **без- (бес-)** has practically the same function as не-, e. g. безопáсный (not dangerous), бесполéзный (useless, of no use).

3) **за-,** which often denotes: begin (to), start (to), e. g. заволновáться, закурúть, зашагáть.

4) **-ость.** Many adjectives may be changed into nouns (always belonging to the feminine gender, and always denoting abstracts) by the addition of -ость to their stem, e. g. слáбый (weak); слáбость (weakness); обязанный (obliged); обязанность (obligation).

5) **-ние or -ение.** Nouns may often be formed from verbal stems by the addition of -ние or -ение, e. g. замечáние (remark), приглашéние (invitation).

6) **-ный or -ной.** Adjectives in -ный or -ной are frequently formed from nouns, e. g. зубнóй (concerning tooth; зубнóй врач), кнúжный (concerning book; кнúжный магазúн).

7) **-ский or -ской.** Adjectives may be formed from nouns by means of -ский or -ской, e. g. пионéрский, городскóй, студéнческий.

8) **-ся.** Verbs may be made reflexive or acquire a passive sense by the addition of the ending -ся, e. g. встречáть (meet) (some-

6

body), встречáться (meet) (one another); писáть (write), писáться (be written).

9) **по-** belongs to the prefixes most frequently used at the formation of perfective verbs.

Many imperfective verbs have corresponding perfective forms prefixed with по- (дýмать / подýмать).

Besides, several imperfective verbs which have either no corresponding perfective form or whose corresponding perfective form is regularly characterized by another prefix or appears as a different verbal form, may be prefixed with по-. In such cases, besides indicating the perfective aspect, по- slightly alters the meaning of the verb, which, then, implies:

a) "begin to" (полюбúть = fall in love; любúть (only ipf.) = love);

b) "a little" (почитáть = read a little; читáть is regularly made perfective by means of the prefix про-).

Added to determinate verbs of motion по- always conveys the meaning of "begin to" (пойтú = begin to go), whereas indeterminate verbs of motion when prefixed with по- take on the meaning of "a little" (полетáть = fly a little).

Most comparative forms may be prefixed with по- in the sense of "a little" (погрóмче = a little louder).

As is seen from some of the above examples, and from several instances in the Dictionary, the permutation of consonants plays a very important part in the Russian language, especially as concerns the conjugation of verbs and the formation of comparative forms. The most important consonant permutations are: г → ж, к → ч, х → ш, т → ч (щ), д → ж (жд), с → ш, з → ж, ст → щ, ск → щ.

The Arrangement of the
RUSSIAN-ENGLISH BASIC DICTIONARY

Grammatical and morphological information is given after the entries for the parts of speech mentioned below.

For nouns: Change of stress is indicated, and irregular forms of declension, including forms with obviously changed consonants, are stated; information is given about the gender and number of words, when this is not clear from their basic forms.

For adjectives: Predicative forms with inserted vowels or irregular stress are given (omitted forms are stressed as the last form indicated). Irregular comparative forms are given after the predicative forms, separated from them by a semicolon.

For verbs: The conjugation of the present tense is given in the 1st pers. sg., the 3rd pers. sg., and the 3rd pers. pl. for all verbs, with the exception of the types in -ать /-аю and -ять /-яю (such as делать, гулять); further, irregular preterite forms and imperative forms are indicated. Separate entries are given for participles, in accordance with the practice of Ожегов: Словарь русского языка. The perfective forms of verbs are invariably given, and for verbs of motion it is stated whether they are determinate or indeterminate. All special syntactic functions of verbs are indicated.

References are given from perfective forms of verbs, from irregular comparative forms and from irregularly inflected forms of nouns, pronouns and numerals.

Idioms are included only when they are considered to be of high frequency, and when their meaning cannot be inferred from the main entries.

For prepositions and various particles with a wide range of meaning semantic variants are illustrated by examples.

8

List of Abbreviations

ab.	about, concerning	ipf.	imperfective
acc.	the accusative case	m.	the masculine gender
adj.	adjective	n.	the neuter gender
adv.	adverb	nom.	the nominative case
comp.	comparative	pers.	person, personal
dat.	the dative case	pf.	perfective
det.	determinate	pl.	the plural
E	all endings stressed	poss.	possessive
etc.	etcetera	prep.	preposition
f.	the feminine gender	pret.	the preterite tense
fut.	the future tense	pron.	pronoun
gen.	the genitive case	sg.	the singular
impers.	impersonal	smb.	somebody
indet.	indeterminate	smth.	something
inf.	infinitive	trans.	transitive
instr.	the instrumental case	vb.	verb
intrans.	intransitive		

The Russian Alphabet

А	а	З	з	П	п	Ч	ч
Б	б	И	и	Р	р	Ш	ш
В	в	Й	й	С	с	Щ	щ
Г	г	К	к	Т	т		ъ
Д	д	Л	л	У	у	Ы	ы
Е	е	М	м	Ф	ф		ь
Ё	ё	Н	н	Х	х	Э	э
Ж	ж	О	о	Ц	ц	Ю	ю
						Я	я

А

^А **а**

    1) *but, while*

    2) *yet*

    3) *and*

^А **а́вгуст** *August*

^А **автобус** *(motor)bus*

^В **а́втор**

    1) *author, authoress, writer, composer*

    2) *originator*

^С **агроно́м** *agriculturist, agronomist*

^В **а́дрес** (*pl.* адреса́) *address*

^С **акаде́мия** *academy*

^В **аккура́тный** (аккура́тен, аккура́тна)

    1) *regular, accurate, punctual*

    2) *careful*

^В **актёр** *actor*

^А **америка́нский** *American*

^А **англи́йский** *English*

^В **англича́нин** (*pl. nom.* англича́не, *gen.* англича́н) *Englishman*

^С **аппара́т**

    1) *apparatus*

    2) *organs*

    3) *staff*

^А **апре́ль** (*m.*) *April*

    арестова́ть *see* **аресто́вывать**

^В **аресто́вывать** / **арестова́ть** (аресту́ю, аресту́ет, аресту́ют) *arrest*

^С **а́рмия** *army, forces*

^А **арти́ст** *artist, actor*

^С **афи́ша** *bill, placard, poster*

^С **аэропо́рт** (в аэропорту́) *airport*

Б

    б *see* **бы**

^в **ба́ба**
    1) *peasant woman*
    2) *woman*
    3) *hag*
    4) *(ab. man) nincompoop*
    сне́жная ба́ба = *snow man*

^А **ба́бушка** (*gen. pl.* ба́бушек) *grandmother, grand-mamma*

^С **база́р**
    1) *market*
    2) *bazaar*

^в **бал** (на балу́; *pl. E*) *ball*

^С **бале́т** *ballet*

^в **балко́н**
    balcony

^С **ба́нка** (*gen. pl.* ба́нок) *jar, pot, tin*

^С **ба́рин** (господа́ *is most frequently used as the pl.; in vulgar language the pl.* ба́ре / ба́ры *gen.* бар *may be used*)
    (in Pre-revolutionary Russia)
    1) *man belonging to the upper strata of society*
    2) *master*
    3) *Your Honour (used by the servants in addressing the master of the house)*

^С **ба́рышня** (*gen. pl.* ба́рышень)
    1) *young, unmarried gentlewoman*
    2) *girl, young lady*
    3) *Miss*

^С **башма́к** (E) *shoe, boot*

^С **ба́шня** (*gen. pl.* ба́шен) *tower*

^в **бе́гать** *(indet. vb. of motion) (ipf.) run*

^в **беда́** (*pl.* бе́ды) *misfortune, trouble, bad luck*

^А **бе́дный** (бе́ден, бедна́, бе́дно, бе́дны) *poor*

^А **бежа́ть** (бегу́, бежи́т, бегу́т) *(det. vb. of motion) (ipf.)*
    1) *run*
    2) *fly (ab. time)*

^А **без** (бе́зо) *(prep. + gen.) without*

без пяти́ шесть (часо́в) = *it is five minutes to six; at five minutes to six*

бе́зо *see* **без**

^A **бе́лый** (бел, бела́, бе́ло́, бе́лы́) *white*

^B **бельё** *linen, underwear, washing*

^A **бе́рег** (на берегу́; *pl.* берега́) *bank, shore, beach*

^B **берёза** *birch*

^B **бере́чь** (берегу́, бережёт, берегу́т; берёг, берегла́, берегло́, берегли́) *(ipf.) take care of*

^A **бесе́да** *conversation, talk*

^B **бесе́довать** (бесе́дую, бесе́дует, бесе́дуют) *(ipf.) talk*

^B **беспоко́ить** (беспоко́ю, беспоко́ит, беспоко́ят) *(ipf.) make anxious, worry, disturb*

^B **библиоте́ка** *library*

^B **биле́т** *ticket*

^C **биоло́гия** *biology*

^A **бить** (бью, бьёт, бьют; бей), **по-, про-, раз-**
  1) *(pf.* по-*) beat*
  2) *(pf.* про-*) strike (ab. clock)*
  3) *(pf.* раз-; разобью́, разобьёт, разобью́т; разбе́й) *break, smash*

^B **благодари́ть** (благодарю́, благодари́т, благодаря́т), **по-** *thank*

^B **благода́рный** (благода́рен, благода́рна) *grateful*

^B **благодаря́** *(prep. + dat.) thanks to, owing to*
  благодаря́ тому́, что… = *thanks to the fact that…*

^B **благоро́дный** (благоро́ден, благоро́дна) *noble*

^B **бледне́ть** (бледне́ю, бледне́ет, бледне́ют), **по-** *turn pale*

^B **бле́дный** (бле́ден, бледна́, бле́дно, бле́дны́)
  1) *pale, wan*
  2) *insipid*

блесну́ть *see* **блесте́ть**

^A **блесте́ть** (блещу́, блести́т, блестя́т *or* бле́щет, бле́щут) / **блесну́ть** (блесну́, блеснёт, блесну́т) *shine, glitter, sparkle*

^A **блестя́щий**
 1) *shining, glittering, sparkling*
 2) *brilliant, fine*
бли́же *see* **бли́зкий**
^A **бли́зкий** (бли́зок, близка́, бли́зко, бли́зки; бли́же) *near, imminent*
^B **бог** (*vocative* бо́же) *god, God*
 сла́ва бо́гу! = *thank God!, thank goodness!*
 не дай бог! = *God forbid!*
 бо́же мой! = *my goodness!*
^B **бога́тство**
 1) *riches*
 2) *richness*
^A **бога́тый** (бога́че) *rich, wealthy*
бога́че *see* **бога́тый**
^C **бо́дрый** (бодр, бодра́, бо́дро, бо́дры) *brisk, cheerful, hale and hearty*
^B **боево́й**
 1) *battle, fighting*
 2) *militant*
 3) *go-ahead, determined*
^B **бое́ц** (*gen.* бойца́) *fighting-man, warrior*
бо́же *see* **бог**
^B **бой** (в бо́е / в бою́; *pl. nom.* бои́, *gen.* боёв) *battle, action*
 взять в бою́ = *take by force*
^B **бок** (в, на, боку́; *pl.* бока́) *side*
^A **бо́лее** *more*
 тем бо́лее = *all the more*
^B **боле́знь** (*f.*) *disease, illness*
^A **боле́ть** (*only in the 3rd pers.:* боли́т, боля́т) (*ipf.*) *ache, hurt*
^C **боло́то** *bog, swamp, morass, marsh*
^B **боль** (*f.*) *pain*
^B **больни́ца** *hospital*
^B **бо́льно** *badly, hard*
 бо́льно уда́рить = *hit hard*
^A **больно́й** (бо́лен, больна́) *sick, diseased, ill*

больно́й вопро́с = a *sore subject*

^A бо́льше

1) (*comp. of* большо́й) *bigger, larger, greater*

2) (*comp. of* мно́го) *more*

^B **большинство́** *majority, most people*

^A **большо́й** *(for predicative forms see* вели́кий; бо́льше*) big, large, great*

^C **бормота́ть** (бормочу́, бормо́чет, бормо́чут) *(ipf.) mutter*

^B **борода́** *(sg. acc.* бо́роду, *gen.* бороды́, *pl. nom.* бо́роды, *gen.* боро́д, *dat.* борода́м*) beard*

^B **боро́ться** (борю́сь, бо́рется, бо́рются) *(ipf.) fight, struggle*

^B **борт** *(pl.* борта́*) side (of a ship)*

вы́бросить за борт = *throw overboard*

^B **борьба́** *(E) struggle, fight*

^B **боти́нок** *(gen.* боти́нка*) boot*

^A **боя́ться** (бою́сь, бои́тся, боя́тся) *(ipf.)* (кого́ / чего́) *fear (smb. / smth.)*

^A **брат** *(pl. nom.* бра́тья, *gen.* бра́тьев*) brother*

двою́родный брат = *cousin*

^A **брать** (беру́, берёт, беру́т; брал, брала́, бра́ло, бра́ли) / **взять** (возьму́, возьмёт, возьму́т; взял, взяла́, взя́ло, взя́ли) *take*

брать себя́ в ру́ки = *pull oneself together*

^B **бра́ться** (беру́сь, берётся, беру́тся; бра́лся, брала́сь, брало́сь, брали́сь) **за** / **взя́ться** (возьму́сь, возьмётся, возьму́тся; взя́лся, взяла́сь, взя́лось, взя́ли́сь) **за**

1) (кого́ / что) *seize (smb. / smth.)*

2) (что) *begin ((to do) smth.)*

^B **брига́да**

1) *brigade*

2) *team*

^C **брить** (бре́ю, бре́ет, бре́ют), **по-** *shave*

^A **бровь** *(f.) (gen. pl.* брове́й*) eyebrow*

^B **броди́ть** (брожу́, бро́дит, бро́дят) *(ipf.) wander, roam, rove*

^A **броса́ть / бро́сить** (бро́шу, бро́сит, бро́сят)
    1) *(кого́ / что or* чем в кого́ / во что*) throw
    (smb. | smth. or smth. at smb. | smth.)*
    2) *(+ inf. or* что*) give up (smth.)*
  бро́сить *see* **броса́ть**
^B **брю́ки** *(only pl.) (gen.* брюк*) trousers*
^A **буди́ть** (бужу́, бу́дит, бу́дят), **про-, раз-**
    1) *(pf.* раз-*) wake, awaken*
    2) *(pf.* про-*) arouse, stir up*
^A **бу́дто** *as if, as though*
  бу́ду *see* **быть**
^A **бу́дущий** *future, to be, to come, next*
  бу́дущее = *the future*
^B **бу́ква** *letter*
^C **бу́лочная** *(adj. used substantively) baker's shop*
^A **бума́га** *paper*
^B **бума́жка** *(gen. pl.* бума́жек*)*
    1) *piece of paper, bit of paper*
    2) *note*
^C **бу́рный** (бу́рен, бурна́, бу́рно)
    1) *stormy, rough*
    2) *impetuous, rapid*
    3) *violent*
^B **бу́ря** *storm, tempest, gale*
^B **буты́лка** *(gen. pl.* буты́лок*) bottle*
^B **буфе́т**
    1) *sideboard*
    2) *refreshment room, buffet*
^A **бы (б)** *(modal particle, used with verbs in the
  preterite tense)*
    1) *should, would*
    2) *should like, would like*
    3) *ought to*
  е́сли бы я знал, я сказа́л бы = *if I had known,
    I would have told you*
  я хоте́л бы уе́хать = *I should like to go away*
  ты бы так и сде́лал! = *you ought to do the
    same thing!*

^A **быва́ть** *(ipf.)*
  1) *be (sometimes, usually)*
  2) *happen, occur, take place*
  как ни в чём не быва́ло = *as if nothing had happened*

^B **бы́вший** *former, late*

^A **бы́стрый** (быстр, быстра́, бы́стро) *quick, rapid, fast, prompt*

^C **быт** (в быту́) *mode of life, life, daily round*

^A **быть** *(the only present-tense form that may be used is the 3rd pers. sg.:* есть; будь; был, была́, бы́ло, бы́ли (не́ был, не была́, не́ было, не́ были); *fut.:* бу́ду, бу́дет, бу́дут) *be*
  у меня́ есть брат = *I have a brother*

^C **бюро́** *(indeclinable n.) bureau, office*

В

^A **в** (во) *(prep. + acc. or the prepositional case)*
  (+ acc.)
  1) *into, in, at, to, for*
  2) *(indicating time) on, at; last*
  3) *(indicating price or measure) at, of, in; not translated*
  (+ the prepositional case)
  1) *in, at*
  2) *(indicating time) in; not translated*
  3) *(indicating distance) not translated*
  4) *(with reference to dress) in*
  войти́ в зда́ние = *go into the building*
  в пя́тницу = 1) *on Friday* 2) *on Fridays* 3) *last Friday*
  места́ в два рубля́ = *seats at two roubles, two-rouble seats*
  стол в два ме́тра = *a table of two metres*
  находи́ться в зда́нии = *be in the building*
  он уе́хал в 1930 году́ = *he left in 1930*
  в двух шага́х от меня́ = *two steps from me*

де́вушка в бе́лом пла́тье = *a girl in a white dress*

ᴮ **ваго́н** *carriage*

ᴬ **ва́жный** (ва́жен, важна́, ва́жно, ва́жны́)
1) *important, significant*
2) *grand, pompous*

вам *see* **вы**

ва́ми *see* **вы**

ᴬ **варе́нье** *jam*

ᶜ **вари́ть** (варю́, ва́рит, ва́рят), **с-**
1) *cook*
2) *boil (trans.)*

вас *see* **вы**

ᴬ **ваш** (*gen.* ва́шего; *f.* ва́ша, *gen.* ва́шей; *n.* ва́ше, *gen.* ва́шего; *pl.* ва́ши, *gen.* ва́ших) *your, yours*

ᶜ **вбега́ть / вбежа́ть** (вбегу́, вбежи́т, вбегу́т) (во что) *run (into smth.)*

вбежа́ть *see* **вбега́ть**

ᴬ **вверх** *up, upwards*
вверх дном = *upside down*

ᶜ **вверху́** *above, overhead*

ᶜ **вдали́** *in the distance*

ᶜ **вдвоём** *two (together)*

ᶜ **вдова́** (*pl.* вдо́вы) *widow*
соло́менная вдова́ = *grass widow*

ᴮ **вдоль** (*prep.* + *gen.*) *along*

ᴬ **вдруг** *suddenly, all of a sudden*

ᶜ **ведро́** (*pl. nom.* вёдра, *gen.* вёдер) *bucket, pail*

ᴬ **ведь** *you see, you know; not translated*

ᴮ **ве́жливый** *polite, courteous*

ᴬ **везде́** *everywhere*

ᴮ **везти́** (везу́, везёт, везу́т; вёз, везла́, везло́, везли́) (*det. vb. of motion*) (*ipf.*) *convey, carry, drive, take*
ему́ везёт = *he is lucky*

ᴬ **век** (на веку́; *pl.* века́)
1) *century*
2) *age*

^в **веле́ть** (велю́, вели́т, веля́т) *(ipf. / pf.; in the pret. only pf.)*
(кому́ / чему́ + *inf.*) *order (smb. / smth. (to do) smth.)*

^А **вели́кий** (вели́к, велика́, вели́ко, вели́ки *or* вели́к, велика́, велико́, велики́; *the predicative forms of the type E are used as the predicative forms of* большо́й *in the sense of* "*too big*", "*too large*")
1) *great*
2) *(only the predicative forms with stressed endings) too big, too large*

^С **великоле́пный** (великоле́пен, великоле́пна)
splendid, magnificent

^А **велосипе́д** *bicycle*

^В **ве́ра**
1) *faith, belief*
2) *trust*

^В **верёвка** *(gen. pl.* верёвок*) rope, cord, string*

^А **ве́рить** (ве́рю, ве́рит, ве́рят) *(ipf.)*
1) (кому́ / чему́) *believe (smb. / smth.), trust (smb. / smth.)*
2) (в кого́ / во что) *believe (in smb. / smth.), have faith (in smb. / smth.)*

верну́ться *see* **возвраща́ться**

^А **ве́рный** (ве́рен, верна́, ве́рно, ве́рны́)
1) *true*
2) *correct, right*

^В **вероя́тно** *probably, likely*

^С **верх** (на верху́; *pl.* верхи́)
1) *top, head*
2) *height, summit*
3) *cover, outside, right side*

^В **ве́рхний**
1) *upper*
2) *outdoor*

^С **верхо́м** *astride, on horseback*

^С **верши́на** *top, summit, crest*

^A весёлый (весел, весела, весело) *merry, gay, cheerful, jovial*

^B весе́нний *spring*

^A весна́ *(pl. nom.* вёсны, *gen.* вёсен*) spring*
весно́й = *in spring*

^A вести́ (веду́, ведёт, веду́т; вёл, вела́, вело́, вели́) *(det. vb. of motion) (ipf.) lead, conduct*
он не уме́ет вести́ себя́ = *he cannot behave himself*

^A весь *(gen.* всего́; *f.* вся, *gen.* всей; *n.* всё, *gen.* всего́; *pl.* все, *gen.* всех*)*
1) *all, the whole*
2) *everybody, everything*
(я жела́ю вам) всего́ хоро́шего = *(I wish you) all the best! good-bye!*
при всём том = *moreover, all the same*

^B весьма́ *highly, greatly*

^A ве́тер *(gen.* ве́тра; на ветру́) *wind*

^B ве́тка *(gen. pl.* ве́ток) *branch, twig*

^A ве́чер *(pl.* вечера́)*
1) *evening*
2) *party, soirée*
ве́чером = *in the evening*

^B вече́рний *evening*

^B ве́чный (ве́чен, ве́чна) *eternal, everlasting*

^C ве́шать / пове́сить (пове́шу, пове́сит, пове́сят) *hang (trans.)*

^A вещь *(f.) (gen. pl.* веще́й) *thing*
взволнова́ться *see* волнова́ться

^A взгляд
1) *look, gaze*
2) *point of view, opinion*

^A взгля́дывать / взгляну́ть (взгляну́, взгля́нет, взгля́нут) (на кого́ / что) *look (at smb. / smth.)*
взгляну́ть *see* взгля́дывать

^C вздох *sigh, deep breath*
вздохну́ть *see* вздыха́ть

^В **вздра́гивать / вздро́гнуть** (вздро́гну, вздро́гнет, вздро́гнут) *startle*

вздро́гнуть *see* **вздра́гивать**

^А **вздыха́ть / вздохну́ть** (вздохну́, вздохнёт, вздохну́т) *sigh*

взойти́ *see* **всходи́ть**

^А **взро́слый** *adult*

^С **взрыв**
1) *explosion*
2) *outburst*

взять *see* **брать**

взя́ться за *see* **бра́ться за**

^А **вид** (в, на, виду́)
1) *air, appearance, look*
2) *view*
3) *sort, kind, species*
на виду́ у всех = *in (plain) sight of everybody*
быть на виду́ = *play a prominent part, be an outstanding figure*
име́ть в виду́ = *bear in mind*
де́лать вид, что = *pretend, feign*

^В **вида́ть, по-, у-**
1) *see*
2) *meet*
3) *experience*

^А **ви́деть** (ви́жу, ви́дит, ви́дят), **у-** *see*

^В **ви́димо** *apparently*

^А **ви́дный** (ви́ден, видна́, ви́дно, ви́дны́)
1) *visible, conspicuous*
2) *eminent, distinguished, prominent*
3) *portly, handsome*
вам хорошо́ ви́дно? = *can you see all right?*

^С **вина́** *(pl.* ви́ны) *fault, guilt*

^А **вино́** *(pl.* ви́на)
1) *wine*
2) *snaps, vodka*

^А **винова́тый**
1) *guilty*

2) *conscience-stricken, apologetic*
винова́т ! = *sorry!*

A висе́ть (вишу́, виси́т, вися́т) *(ipf.) hang (intrans.)*
C ви́шня *(gen. pl.* ви́шен*)*
  1) *cherry, cherries*
  2) *cherry(-tree)*
A включа́ть / включи́ть (включу́, включи́т, включа́т)
  1) *include*
  2) *engage, switch on*
  включи́ть *see* включа́ть
B вкус *taste*
B вку́сный (вку́сен, вку́сна) *delicious*
C владе́ть (владе́ю, владе́ет, владе́ют) *(ipf.)*
  1) (кем / чем) *own (smb. | smth.)*
  2) (кем/чем) *be able to use (smb. | smth.)*
  3) (чем) *be master (of smth.)*
B власть *(f.) (gen. pl.* власте́й*) power, authority*
C влеза́ть / влезть (вле́зу, вле́зет, вле́зут; влез, вле́зла, вле́зло, вле́зли)
  (на что) *climb (smth.),* (во что) *climb (into, through, smth.)*
  влезть *see* влеза́ть
B влия́ние *influence*
  влюби́ться *see* влюбля́ться
B влюблённый
  1) (в кого́ / во что) *in love (with smb. | smth.)*
  2) *amorous*
  3) *lover*
B влюбля́ться / влюби́ться (влюблю́сь, влю́бится, влю́бятся)
  (в кого́ / во что) *fall in love (with smb. | smth.)*
A вме́сте *together*
  вме́сте с тем = *at the same time*
A вме́сто *(prep.* + *gen.) instead of*
  вмеша́ться *see* вме́шиваться
B вме́шиваться / вмеша́ться (во что) *interfere (in smth.)*

22

^B **внеза́пно** *suddenly, all of a sudden*
   внести́ *see* **вноси́ть**
^C **вне́шний** *outward, external, outer*
^B **вниз** *down, downwards*
^A **внизу́** *below, downstairs*
^A **внима́ние** *attention*
^A **внима́тельный** (внима́телен, внима́тельна) *attentive, intent*
^B **вновь** *anew, again, once more*
^C **вноси́ть** (вношу́, вно́сит, вно́сят) / **внести́** (внесу́, внесёт, внесу́т; внёс, внесла́, внесло́, внесли́)
   1) (кого́ / что во что) *carry (smb. / smth. into smth.)*
   2) *pay*
   3) *move, put forward*
   4) (что во что) *bring (smth. into smth.), introduce (smth. into smth.)*
^C **внук** *grandson*
^B **вну́тренний** *inside, interior, internal, inner*
^B **внутри́**
   1) *(adv.) inside*
   2) *(prep. + gen.) inside, within*
^A **вну́чка** *(gen. pl.* вну́чек*) granddaughter*
   во *see* **в**
^C **во́время** *in time, opportunely*
^B **во́все не** *not at all*
   во-вторы́х *see* **второ́й**
^A **вода́** *(sg. acc.* во́ду, *gen.* воды́, *pl.* во́ды*) water*
^B **води́ть** (вожу́, во́дит, во́дят) *(indet. vb. of motion) (ipf.) lead, conduct*
^B **во́дка** *vodka*
^C **воева́ть** (вою́ю, вою́ет, вою́ют) *(ipf.) wage war, fight*
^A **вое́нный**
   1) *military, war*
   2) *(used substantively) soldier, serviceman*
   возврати́ться *see* **возвраща́ться**
^A **возвраща́ться** / **возврати́ться** (возвращу́сь, воз-

вратится, возвратятся) *or* **вернуться** (вернусь, вернётся, вернутся) *return*

^A **воздух** *air*

^C **возить** (вожу, возит, возят) *(indet. vb. of motion) (ipf.) convey, drive*

^A **возле**
1) *(adv.) near, beside*
2) *(prep. + gen.) by, near, beside*

^A **возможность** *(f.) possibility, opportunity, chance*

^A **возможный** (возможен, возможна) *possible, feasible*

^B **возникать / возникнуть** *(only in the 3rd pers.:* возникнет, возникнут; возник, возникла, возникло, возникли) *arise, appear*

возникнуть *see* **возникать**

^B **возражать / возразить** (возражу, возразит, возразят) *object, raise an objection*

возразить *see* **возражать**

^B **возраст** *age*

^A **война** *(pl.* войны) *war*

войти *see* **входить**

^B **вокзал** *(railway) station*

^A **вокруг**
1) *(adv.) around*
2) *(prep. + gen.) round, around*

^C **волк** *(gen. pl.* волков) *wolf*

^B **волна** *(pl. nom.* волны, *dat.* волнам) *wave*

^B **волнение**
1) *(rough) sea*
2) *agitation, emotion*

^A **волноваться** (волнуюсь, волнуется, волнуются), **вз-**
1) *be rough (ab. the sea)*
2) *be agitated, be upset*

^A **волос** *(pl. gen.* волос, *dat.* волосам) *hair*

^C **волшебный** (волшебен, волшебна)
1) *magic*
2) *enchanting*

^В во́ля
  1) *will*
  2) *(old) liberty*
^А вон
  1) *out, away*
  2) *there, over there*
^А вообще́
  1) *in general, generally, altogether*
  2) *(in connection with negations) at all*
во-пе́рвых *see* пе́рвый
^А вопро́с *question, matter, issue*
^С вор *(gen. pl.* воро́в*) thief*
^А воро́та *(n., only pl.; gen.* воро́т*)*
  1) *gate, gates*
  2) *goal*
^В воротни́к *(gen.* воротника́*) collar*
^В восемна́дцать *(gen.* восемна́дцати*) eighteen*
^А во́семь *(gen.* восьми́, *instr.* восьмью́ / восемью́*)*
  eight
воскли́кнуть *see* восклица́ть
^В восклица́ть / воскли́кнуть (воскли́кну, воскли́к-
  нет, воскли́кнут) *exclaim, cry out*
^А воскресе́нье *Sunday*
воспита́ть *see* воспи́тывать
^В воспи́тывать / воспита́ть
  1) *bring up, educate*
  2) (что в ком) *foster, cultivate (smth. in smb.)*
  воспи́танный ребёнок = *a well-behaved child*
воспо́льзоваться *see* по́льзоваться
^В воспомина́ние
  1) *recollection, memory*
  2) *(pl.) memoirs*
^В восто́к *east*
^В восто́рг *enthusiasm, delight, rapture*
восходи́ть *see* всходи́ть
^А восьмо́й *eighth*
^А вот
  1) *here is*

2) *what (a)*

он вот-во́т придёт = *he will come in a moment*

вот ещё! = *indeed! I like that!*

вот и всё = *and that's all*

^A **впервы́е** *for the first time*

^A **вперёд** *forward*

часы́ иду́т вперёд = *the clock is fast*

^A **впереди́**

1) *(adv.) in front, before*

2) *(prep. + gen.) in front of, before*

^A **впечатле́ние** *impression*

^B **вполне́** *quite, fully*

^A **впро́чем** *however, though*

^A **враг** *(E) enemy*

^A **врать** (вру, врёт, врут; врал, врала́, вра́ло, вра́ли), **на-, со-** *lie, tell lies*

^A **врач** *(E) physician, doctor*

^C **вре́дный** (вре́ден, вредна́, вре́дно, вре́дны) *harmful, injurious*

^A **вре́мя** *(n.) (sg. gen., dat., the prepositional case* вре́мени, *instr.* вре́менем, *pl. nom.* времена́, *gen.* времён, *dat.* времена́м*) time*

в то вре́мя как = *while, whereas*

тем вре́менем = *meanwhile*

^B **вро́де** *(prep. + gen.) like, such as*

^A **всё**

1) *(n. of* весь*) all, everything*

2) *(adv.) always, all the time*

всё же = *all the same, nevertheless*

всё ещё = *still*

^A **всегда́** *always*

^B **всего́** *in all, altogether*

всего́-на́всего = *in all*

^A **всё-таки** *for all that, still, nevertheless, all the same*

^A **вска́кивать / вскочи́ть** (вскочу́, вско́чит, вско́чат)

1) (на кого / что) *jump (on (to), into, smb. / smth.)*

2) *jump up, leap up*

вскипе́ть *see* **кипе́ть**

A **вско́ре** *soon, shortly after*

вскочи́ть *see* **вска́кивать**

B **вслед**

> 1) *(prep. + dat.)* смотре́ть вслед кому́-нибудь
> *follow somebody with one's eyes*
>
> 2) *(adv.)* (за кем / чем) *after (smb. / smth.)*

C **вслух** *aloud*

A **вспомина́ть** / **вспо́мнить** (вспо́мню, вспо́мнит, вспо́мнят)

> (кого́ / что *or* о ком / чём) *remember (smb. / smth.), think of (smb. / smth.)*

вспо́мнить *see* **вспомина́ть**

B **вспы́хивать** / **вспы́хнуть** (вспы́хну, вспы́хнет, вспы́хнут)

> 1) *take fire, blaze up*
>
> 2) *break out*
>
> 3) *blush*

вспы́хнуть *see* **вспы́хивать**

A **встава́ть** (встаю́, встаёт, встаю́т) / **встать** (вста́ну, вста́нет, вста́нут) *get up, rise*

встать *see* **встава́ть**

встре́тить *see* **встреча́ть**

A **встре́ча**

> 1) *meeting, reception*
>
> 2) *match*
>
> встре́ча Но́вого го́да = *New Year's eve party*

A **встреча́ть** / **встре́тить** (встре́чу, встре́тит, встре́тят)

> 1) *meet*
>
> 2) (кого́) *receive (smb.)*
>
> встре́тить Пе́рвое ма́я = *celebrate the First of May*

A **вступа́ть** / **вступи́ть** (вступлю́, всту́пит, всту́пят) (во что) *enter ((into) smth.)*

вступи́ть *see* **вступа́ть**

C **всходи́ть** (всхожу́, всхо́дит, всхо́дят) *or* **вос-** /

взойти́ (взойду́, взойдёт, взойду́т; взошёл, взошла́, взошло́, взошли́)
1) *(ipf.* всходи́ть*)* (на что) *mount (smth.), climb (smth.),* (по чему́) *mount (smth.)*
2) *(ipf.* восходи́ть*) rise (ab. the sun)*
3) *(ipf.* всходи́ть*) spring, sprout*

^B **всю́ду** *everywhere*

вся *see* **весь**

^A **вся́кий**
1) *any, every*
2) *all sorts of*
3) *anybody, everybody*

^A **вто́рник** *Tuesday*

^A **второ́й** *second*

во-вторы́х = *in the second place, secondly*

в-тре́тьих *see* **тре́тий**

^C **вуз** *(abbreviation of:* вы́сшее уче́бное заведе́ние*) higher educational institution*

^B **вход**
1) *entrance*
2) *entry*

^A **входи́ть** (вхожу́, вхо́дит, вхо́дят) / **войти́** (войду́, войдёт, войду́т; вошёл, вошла́, вошло́, вошли́)

(во что) *enter (smth.), go into (smth.), be a member (of smth.), take part (in smth.)*

^A **вчера́** *yesterday*

^C **вчера́шний** *yesterday's*

^A **вы** *(acc., gen., the prepositional case* вас, *dat.* вам, *instr.* ва́ми*) (pers. pron.) you*

^A **выбега́ть** / **вы́бежать** (вы́бегу, вы́бежит, вы́бегут) *run out*

вы́бежать *see* **выбега́ть**

^A **выбира́ть** / **вы́брать** (вы́беру, вы́берет, вы́берут)
1) *choose, select, pick out*
2) *elect*

^B **вы́бор**
1) *choice, selection, option*

2) *(only pl.) election, elections*

^C **выбра́сывать** / **вы́бросить** (вы́брошу, вы́бросит, вы́бросят) *throw out, discard*

вы́брать *see* **выбира́ть**

вы́бросить *see* **выбра́сывать**

вы́вести *see* **выводи́ть**

^В **выводи́ть** (вывожу́, выво́дит, выво́дят) / **вы́вести** (вы́веду, вы́ведет, вы́ведут; вы́вел, вы́вела, вы́вело, вы́вели)

    1) *lead out, take out, help out*

    2) *remove*

    3) (кого́ из чего́) *exclude (smb. from smth.)*

    4) *conclude, infer*

вы́гладить *see* **гла́дить**

^В **вы́глядеть** (вы́гляжу, вы́глядит, вы́глядят) *(ipf.) look*

^В **выдава́ть** (выдаю́, выдаёт, выдаю́т; выдава́й) / **вы́дать** (вы́дам, вы́дашь, вы́даст, вы́дадим, вы́дадите, вы́дадут; вы́дай)

    1) *hand, give, distribute*

    2) *give away, betray*

вы́дать *see* **выдава́ть**

вы́держать *see* **выде́рживать**

^В **выде́рживать** / **вы́держать** (вы́держу, вы́держит, вы́держат) *bear, stand, endure*

    вы́держать экза́мен = *pass an exam*

^З **выезжа́ть** / **вы́ехать** (вы́еду, вы́едет, вы́едут) *leave, drive out*

вы́ехать *see* **выезжа́ть**

вы́звать *see* **вызыва́ть**

^А **вызыва́ть** / **вы́звать** (вы́зову, вы́зовет, вы́зовут)

    1) *call, send for*

    2) *challenge*

    3) *summon*

    4) *provoke, call forth, excite*

вы́играть *see* **вы́игрывать**

^C **вы́игрывать** / **вы́играть** *win, gain*

вы́йти *see* **выходи́ть**

A выключа́ть / вы́ключить (вы́ключу, вы́ключит, вы́ключат)
   1) *turn off, switch off*
   2) *cut off, exclude*
вы́ключить *see* выключа́ть
вы́красить *see* кра́сить
вы́купаться *see* купа́ться
B вылеза́ть / вы́лезть (вы́лезу, вы́лезет, вы́лезут; вы́лез, вы́лезла, вы́лезло, вы́лезли)
   1) *climb out, crawl out*
   2) *(only in the 3rd pers.) peep out (ab. hair)*
вы́лезть *see* вылеза́ть
C вылета́ть / вы́лететь (вы́лечу, вы́летит, вы́летят)
   fly out, take off
вы́лететь *see* вылета́ть
C вылива́ть / вы́лить (вы́лью, вы́льет, вы́льют; вы́лей)
   (что из чего́) pour (smth. out of smth.)
вы́лить *see* вылива́ть
вы́мыть *see* мыть
вы́нести *see* выноси́ть
B вынима́ть / вы́нуть (вы́ну, вы́нет, вы́нут) *take out, pull out*
B выноси́ть (выношу́, выно́сит, выно́сят) / вы́нести (вы́несу, вы́несет, вы́несут; вы́нес, вы́несла, вы́несло, вы́несли)
   1) *carry out, take away*
   2) *make (note), receive (impression)*
   3) *pass (sentence, resolution)*
   4) *stand, endure*
вы́нуть *see* вынима́ть
вы́пить *see* пить
вы́полнить *see* выполня́ть
A выполня́ть / вы́полнить (вы́полню, вы́полнит, вы́полнят) *implement, fulfil, carry out, execute*
B выпуска́ть / вы́пустить (вы́пущу, вы́пустит, вы́пустят)
   1) *let out, release, free*

2) *turn out, put on the market, publish*

вы́пустить *see* **выпуска́ть**

A **выража́ть / вы́разить** (вы́ражу, вы́разит, вы́-
разят) *express*

вы́разить *see* **выража́ть**

вы́расти *see* **расти́**

вы́рваться *see* **вырыва́ться**

вы́ругать *see* **руга́ть**

C **вырыва́ться / вы́рваться** (вы́рвусь, вы́рвется,
вы́рвутся)
1) *(only in the 3rd pers.) be torn away*
2) *(only in the 3rd pers.) escape, burst (ab.
scream, etc.)*
3) *break loose*

B **выска́кивать / вы́скочить** (вы́скочу, вы́скочит,
вы́скочат) *jump out, leap out*

вы́скочить *see* **выска́кивать**

A **высо́кий** (высо́к, высока́, высоко́, высоки́;
вы́ше) *high, tall, lofty*

B **высота́** *(pl.* высо́ты*)*
1) *height, altitude*
2) *eminence, ridge, hill*

B **вы́ставка** *(gen. pl.* вы́ставок*) exhibition, show,
display*

вы́стирать *see* **стира́ть**

C **вы́стрел** *shot*

вы́строить *see* **стро́ить**

A **выступа́ть / вы́ступить** (вы́ступлю, вы́ступит,
вы́ступят)
1) *come forward, advance*
2) *appear, speak (at a meeting)*

вы́ступить *see* **выступа́ть**

B **вы́сший**
1) *highest*
2) *supreme*
3) *higher*

вы́тащить *see* **тащи́ть**

вы́тереть *see* **вытира́ть**

^C **вытира́ть / вы́тереть** (вы́тру, вы́трет, вы́трут;
вы́тер, вы́терла, вы́терло, вы́терли)
1) *wipe*
2) *wear threadbare*
вы́трясти *see* **трясти́**
вы́учить *see* **учи́ть**
вы́учиться *see* **учи́ться**
^B **вы́ход**
1) *going out*
2) *outlet, way out, exit*
^A **выходи́ть** (выхожу́, выхо́дит, выхо́дят) / **вы́йти**
(вы́йду, вы́йдет, вы́йдут; вы́шел, вы́шла,
вы́шло, вы́шли)
1) *go out*
2) *appear, be out*
3) *run out*
де́ло не вы́шло = *it turned out badly*
окно́ выхо́дит на у́лицу = *the room overlooks
the street*
вы́чистить *see* **чи́стить**
вы́ше *see* **высо́кий**

Г

^A **газе́та** *newspaper*
^B **га́лстук** *tie, necktie*
^C **гаси́ть** (гашу́, га́сит, га́сят), **за-, по-** *put out,
extinguish*
^A **где** *where*
^C **где́-нибудь** *somewhere, anywhere*
^A **где́-то** *somewhere*
^B **геогра́фия** *geography*
^C **гео́лог** *geologist*
^C **герма́нский** *German*
^A **геро́й** *hero*
^B **глава́** (*pl.* гла́вы)
1) *head, chief*
2) *chapter*

^A **гла́вный** *main, chief, principal*

^C **гла́дить** (гла́жу, гла́дит, гла́дят), **вы́-, по-**
1) *(pf. вы́-, по-) iron, press*
2) *(pf. по-) stroke*

^A **глаз** (в глазу́; *pl. nom.* глаза́, *gen.* глаз) *eye*
смотре́ть во все глаза́ = *be all eyes*
за его́ глаза́ = *behind his back*
на его́ глаза́х = *before his eyes*

^C **глота́ть / глотну́ть** (глотну́, глотнёт, глотну́т)
1) *swallow*
2) *gulp, choke down*

глотну́ть *see* **глота́ть**

глу́бже *see* **глубо́кий**

^B **глубина́** *(pl.* глуби́ны*) depth*

^A **глубо́кий** (глубо́к, глубока́, глубо́ко́, глубо́ки́; глу́бже) *deep, profound*

^A **глу́пый** (глуп, глупа́, глу́по) *foolish, stupid, silly*

^B **глухо́й** (глух, глуха́, глу́хо; глу́ше)
1) *deaf*
2) *dull, hollow, muffled, toneless*
3) *out-of-the-way, remote*

глу́ше *see* **глухо́й**

^A **гляде́ть** (гляжу́, гляди́т, глядя́т), **по-** *look, peer, gaze*
того́ и гляди́ пойдёт дождь = *I'm afraid it may begin to rain (any moment)*

^C **гнать** (гоню́, го́нит, го́нят; гнал, гнала́, гна́ло, гна́ли) *(ipf.)*
1) *drive, turn out*
2) *pursue, chase*
3) *distil*

^B **гнев** *anger*

^A **говори́ть** (говорю́, говори́т, говоря́т) / **сказа́ть** (скажу́, ска́жет, ска́жут)
1) *(only ipf.) speak, talk*
2) *(ipf. and pf.) say, tell*
не говоря́ уже́ о деньга́х = *to say nothing of money, not to mention money*

и́на́че говоря́ = *in other words*

A **год** (в году́; *pl. nom.* го́ды / года́, *gen.* годо́в)
(лет *is used as the gen. pl. after numerals above*
четы́ре, *after composite numbers ending in
numerals above* четы́ре, *and after adverbs indicating quantity) year*
с Но́вым го́дом! = *A Happy New Year!*

A **голова́** *(sg. acc.* го́лову, *gen.* головы́, *pl. nom.*
го́ловы, *gen.* голо́в, *dat.* голова́м) *head*

B **го́лод** *(gen.* го́лода / го́лоду) *hunger*

A **го́лос** *(pl.* голоса́)*
1) *voice*
2) *part*

A **голубо́й** *blue, light blue, pale blue*

C **го́лубь** *(m.) (gen. pl.* голубе́й) *pigeon, dove*

B **го́лый** (гол, гола́, го́ло) *naked, bare*

A **гора́** *(sg. acc.* го́ру, *gen.* горы́, *pl. nom.* го́ры,
dat. гора́м) *mountain*

A **гора́здо** *(before comp.) much, far*

B **горди́ться** (горжу́сь, горди́тся, гордя́тся) *(ipf.)*
(кем / чем) *be proud (of smb. / smth.), be con-
ceited (about smb. / smth.)*

B **го́рдый** (горд, горда́, го́рдо, го́рды)
1) *proud*
2) *majestic*

B **го́ре** *grief, sorrow, misfortune*

A **горе́ть** (горю́, гори́т, горя́т), **с-** *burn, be on fire, shine*

B **го́рло** *throat*

A **го́род** *(pl.* города́) *town, city*
жить за́ городом = *live in the country*

B **го́рький** (го́рек, горька́, го́рько) *bitter*

A **горя́чий** (горя́ч, горяча́)
1) *hot*
2) *ardent, fervent*
горя́чее вре́мя = *a very busy time*

B **господи́н** *(pl. nom.* господа́, *gen.* госпо́д)
1) *gentleman*
2) *Mr.*

3) *master*

^в **госпожа** *(E)*
   1) *Mrs., Miss*
   2) *lady, mistress*

^в **гостиница** *hotel*

^А **гость** *(m.) (gen. pl.* гостей*) visitor, guest*
   идти в гости = *go on a visit*
   я вернусь из гостей = *I have just returned from a visit*

^в **государство** *state*

^А **готовить** (готовлю, готовит, готовят) *(ipf.)*
   1) *prepare, make ready*
   2) *cook*

^А **готовый** *ready*
   готовое пальто = *a ready-made coat*

^в **гражданин** *(pl. nom.* граждане*, gen.* граждан*)*
   1) *citizen*
   2) *Sir*

^с **гражданка** *(gen. pl.* гражданок*)*
   1) *citizen*
   2) *Mrs.*

^с **гражданский**
   1) *civil*
   2) *civic*
   3) *civilian*

^в **граница**
   1) *boundary, border, frontier*
   2) *limit*
   уехать за границу = *go abroad*
   жить за границей = *live abroad*

^с **греметь** (гремлю, гремит, гремят) *(ipf.) thunder, clatter*

^с **греть** (грею, греет, греют) *(ipf.)*, **на-, со-**
   1) *give out warmth*
   2) *warm, heat, keep warm*

^с **гриб** *(E) fungus, mushroom*

^с **грипп** *influenza*

^с **гроза** *(pl.* грозы*) thunderstorm*

^в **грозить** (грожу, грозит, грозят), **по-, при-**

1) *(pf.* по-*) threaten (by means of gesture(s))*

2) *(pf.* при-*) (*чем*) threaten (with smth.)*

^C **гром** *thunder*

^B **грома́дный** (грома́ден, грома́дна) *huge, enormous, immense*

^A **гро́мкий** (гро́мок, громка́, гро́мко; гро́мче) *loud*

гро́мче *see* **гро́мкий**

^B **гру́бый** (груб, груба́, гру́бо) *rough, coarse, rude*

^A **грудь** *(f.) (gen. pl.* груде́й*)*

1) *breast*

2) *chest*

3) *bosom*

^C **грузови́к** *(E) lorry*

^A **гру́ппа** *group*

^A **гру́стный** (гру́стен, грустна́, гру́стно) *melancholy, sad*

^A **грязь** *(f.)* (в грязи́)

1) *dirt, filth*

2) *mud*

^A **губа́** *(pl. nom.* гу́бы, *dat.* губа́м*) lip*

^C **губерна́тор** *governor*

^C **губе́рния** *province*

^C **гуде́ть** (гужу́, гуди́т, гудя́т) *(ipf.) buzz, drone, hoot, hunk*

^A **гуля́ть, по-** *take a walk, stroll*

^A **густо́й** (густ, густа́, гу́сто, гу́сты; гу́ще)

1) *thick*

2) *dense*

гу́ще *see* **густо́й**

Д

^A **да**

1) *yes*

2) *(in connection with vb. in the present tense) translated by means of the imperative mood*

3) *(old) and*

да здра́вствует на́ша а́рмия! = *long live our army!*

^A **дава́ть** (даю́, даёт, даю́т; дава́й) / **дать** (дам, дашь, даст, дади́м, дади́те, даду́т; дай; дал, дала́, да́ло, да́ли (не́ дал, не дала́, не́ дало, не́ дали)) *give*

давай бе́гать! = *come on, let us run!*

^A **давно́**
1) *long ago*
2) *for a long time*

^A **да́же** *even*

^B **да́лее**
1) *further, later*
2) *forth*

^A **далёкий** (далёк, далека́, далёко́, далёки́; да́льше)
1) *distant, remote*
2) *long (ab. distance)*

далеко́ не = *far from (being)*

^B **дальне́йший** *further, subsequent*

в дальне́йшем = 1) *later on, in future* 2) *below*

^B **да́льний** *distant, remote, long*

без да́льних слов = *without further ado*

^A **да́льше**
1) *see* **далёкий**
2) *(adv.) farther, further*

^B **да́ма**
1) *lady*
2) *partner*
3) *queen (in cards)*

^C **да́нный** *given, present*

да́нные = *data, facts*

^B **дари́ть** (дарю́, да́рит, да́рят), **по-** *give, make a present of*

дать *see* **дава́ть**

^A **да́ча** *cottage (in the country)*

^A **два** *(f.* две; *gen., the prepositional case* двух, *dat.* двум, *instr.* двумя́*) two*

^A **два́дцать** *(gen.* двадцати́*) twenty*

^C **два́жды** *twice*

две *see* **два**

^A **двенáдцать** *(gen.* двенáдцати*) twelve*

^A **дверь** *(f.) (gen. pl.* дверéй*) door*

^A **двéсти** *(gen.* двухсóт, *dat.* двумстáм, *instr.* двумястáми, *the prepositional case* двухстáх*) two hundred*

^A **двúгаться** (двúжусь, двúжется, двúжутся *or* двúгаюсь, двúгается, двúгаются) / **двúнуться** (двúнусь, двúнется, двúнутся) *move*

^A **движéние**
    1) *motion, movement*
    2) *traffic*
  двúнуться *see* **двúгаться**

^A **двóе** *(gen.* двоúх*) two*

^A **двор** *(gen.* дворá*)*
    1) *court, courtyard*
    2) *(peasant) household, farmstead*
  на дворé хóлодно = *it is cold out of doors*

^B **дворéц** *(gen.* дворцá*) palace*

^C **дворянúн** *(pl. nom.* дворя́не, *gen.* дворя́н*)*
    1) *nobleman*
    2) *man belonging to the gentry*

  двум *see* **два**

  двумстáм *see* **двéсти**

  двумя́ *see* **два**

  двумястáми *see* **двéсти**

  двух *see* **два**

  двухсóт *see* **двéсти**

  двухстáх *see* **двéсти**

^A **дéвочка** *(gen. pl.* дéвочек*) (little) girl*

^A **дéвушка** *(gen. pl.* дéвушек*) girl, lass*

^B **девчóнка** *(gen. pl.* девчóнок*) girl, thing, kid*

^B **девянóсто** *(gen., dat., instr., the prepositional case* девянóста*) ninety*

^A **девя́тый** *ninth*

^A **дéвять** *(gen.* девятú*) nine*

^A **дед** *grandfather*
  дед-морóз = *Grandfather Frost, Santa Claus*

^C **дéдушка** *(gen. pl.* дéдушек*) grandfather*

^A **дежу́рный** *(adj. used substantively)*
   1) *(person) on duty*
   2) *monitor*

^B **де́йствие**
   1) *effect*
   2) *action, operation*
   3) *act*

^A **действи́тельно**
   1) *really*
   2) *indeed*

^B **де́йствовать** (де́йствую, де́йствует, де́йствуют),
   по-
   1) *(only ipf.) act, operate, function, work, run*
   2) *(pf. по-)* (на кого́ / что) *have an effect (on
      smb. / smth.)*

^A **дека́брь** *(gen. декабря́) December*

^A **де́лать, с-** *make, do*

^B **де́латься, с-** *become, get, grow*

^C **дели́ть** (делю́, де́лит, де́лят), **по-, раз-**
   1) *(pf. по-, раз-) divide*
   2) *(pf. раз-) divide (mathematics), divide up*
   3) *(pf. раз-)* (что с кем) *share (smb.'s grief,
      joy, etc.)*

^A **де́ло** *(pl. дела́)*
   1) *affair, business, work*
   2) *cause*
   3) *deed, act*
   4) *(only pl.) things*
   5) *matter*
   как дела́? = *how are you?*
   в чём де́ло? = *what is the matter?*
   то и де́ло = *continuously*
   на са́мом де́ле = *actually*

^C **демократи́ческий** *democratic*

^A **день** *(gen. дня) day*
   днём = *in the day-time*
   на днях = 1) *one of these days* 2) *the other day*

A **де́ньги** *(only pl.)* *(gen.* де́нег, *dat.* деньга́м)
  money

C **дереве́нский** *rural*

A **дере́вня** *(gen. pl.* дереве́нь) *village*
  жить в дере́вне = *live in the country*

A **де́рево** *(pl. nom.* дере́вья, *gen.* дере́вьев)
  1) *tree*
  2) *wood*

B **деревя́нный** *wooden*

A **держа́ть** *(ipf.)* (держу́, де́ржит, де́ржат) *hold,*
  keep
  держа́ть себя́ в рука́х = *control oneself*

B **держа́ться** (держу́сь, де́ржится, де́ржатся)
  1) (за что) *hold (on to smth.)*
  2) *behave*
  3) (чего́) *adhere (to smth.), stick (to smth.)*

B **деся́ток** *(gen.* деся́тка) *ten (of the same sort),*
  (only pl.) dozens, scores

A **деся́тый** *tenth*

A **де́сять** *(gen.* десяти́) *ten*

A **де́ти** *(pl.)* *(gen.* дете́й, *dat.* де́тям, *instr.* деть-
  ми́, *the prepositional case* де́тях) *children*

A **де́тский** *child's, children's, infantile*

A **де́тство** *childhood*

  деше́вле *see* **дешёвый**

B **дешёвый** (дёшев, дешева́, дёшево; деше́вле)
  cheap, low

B **дива́н** *sofa*

B **ди́кий** (дик, дика́, ди́ко)
  1) *wild*
  2) *savage*

A **дире́ктор** *(pl.* директора́)
  1) *director, manager*
  2) *head, principal*

C **длина́** *length*

A **дли́нный** (дли́нен, длинна́, дли́нно)
  1) *long, lengthy*
  2) *too long*

^A для *(prep.* + *gen.)*
    1) *for*
    2) *to*

^C дневни́к *(E) diary*
    днём *see* день

^A дно *(pl. nom.* до́нья, *gen.* до́ньев*) bottom*

^A до *(prep.* + *gen.)*
    1) *to, as far as*
    2) *under, up to*
    3) *before*
    доба́вить *see* добавля́ть

^A добавля́ть / доба́вить (доба́влю, доба́вит, доба́вят) *add*

^C добега́ть / добежа́ть (добегу́, добежи́т, добегу́т)
    (до чего́) *run (as far as smth.)*
    добежа́ть *see* добега́ть

^B добива́ться / доби́ться (добью́сь, добьётся, добью́тся) (чего́) *obtain (smth.), achieve (smth.)*

^B добира́ться / добра́ться (доберу́сь, доберётся, доберу́тся; добра́лся, добрала́сь, добра́лось, добра́ли́сь)
    (до кого́ / чего́) *reach (smb. | smth.)*
    доби́ться *see* добива́ться
    добра́ться *see* добира́ться

^C добро́ *(something) good*
    добро́ пожа́ловать! = *welcome!*

^A до́брый (добр, добра́, до́бро, до́бры́) *good, kind*
    в до́брый час! = *good luck!*
    чего́ до́брого = *may…, for all I know*
    дове́рить *see* доверя́ть

^C доверя́ть / дове́рить (дове́рю, дове́рит, дове́рят)
    (кому́ / чему́ кого́ / что) *entrust (smb. | smth. to smb. | smth.)*
    довести́ *see* доводи́ть

^C доводи́ть (довожу́, дово́дит, дово́дят) / довести́ (доведу́, доведёт, доведу́т; довёл, довела́, довело́, довели́)
    (кого́ / что до кого́ / чего́) *lead (smb. | smth.*

as far as, up to, smb. | smth.), lead, accompany
(smb. | smth. to smb. | smth.)
довести́ де́ло до его́ све́дения = *inform him*
of the matter

A **дово́льно**
    1) *rather, fairly*
    2) (чего́) *enough (of smth.)*

A **дово́льный** (дово́лен, дово́льна) *satisfied, content*

  догада́ться *see* **дога́дываться**

A **дога́дываться** / **догада́ться** *guess*

  догна́ть *see* **догоня́ть**

B **догова́риваться** / **договори́ться** (договорю́сь, до-
    говори́тся, договоря́тся)
    (о чём) *arrange (smth.)*

C **догово́р** *agreement, treaty*

  договори́ться *see* **догова́риваться**

C **догоня́ть** / **догна́ть** (догоню́, дого́нит, дого́нят;
    догна́л, догнала́, догна́ло, догна́ли) *catch up*
    with, overtake

C **доезжа́ть** / **дое́хать** (дое́ду, дое́дет, дое́дут)
    (до чего́) *drive (as far as smth.), reach (smth.)*
    (driving)

  дое́хать *see* **доезжа́ть**

C **дождли́вый** *rainy*

A **дождь** *(gen.* дождя́*) rain*
    дождь идёт = *it is raining*

  дойти́ *see* **доходи́ть**

  доказа́ть *see* **дока́зывать**

B **дока́зывать** / **доказа́ть** (докажу́, дока́жет, до-
    ка́жут) *prove*

C **докла́д**
    1) *lecture, paper*
    2) *report*

B **до́ктор** *(pl.* доктора́*)*
    1) *doctor, physician*
    2) *doctor (person who has taken a doctor's degree)*

B **докуме́нт** *document*

B **долг**

1) *(only sg.)* duty

2) *(*в долгу́; *pl. E)* debt

^A **до́лгий** (до́лог, долга́, до́лго; до́льше *or* до́лее) *long*

^A **до́лжен** (должна́) *(used as subjective complement in sentences whose verb is a form of* быть; *the latter is omitted in the present tense)*

1) *(followed by inf.)* must, have to, ought to

2) *(*что кому́ / чему́*)* owe *(smth. to smb. / smth.)*

мы должны́ уйти́ = *we must go*

он до́лжен был уйти́ = *he had to go*

он мне до́лжен два рубля́ = *he owes me two roubles*

должно́ быть = *(very) probably*

^C **доли́на** *valley*

до́льше *see* до́лгий

^B **до́ля** *(gen. pl.* долей*)*

1) *part, portion*

2) *fate, lot*

^A **дом** *(pl.* дома́*) house*

^A **до́ма** *at home*

^B **дома́шний**

1) *house, home*

2) *domestic*

^B **до́мик** *little house, small house*

^A **домо́й** *home*

донести́сь *see* доноси́ться

^B **доноси́ться** *(only in the 3rd pers.:* доно́сится, доно́сятся*) /* **донести́сь** *(only in the 3rd pers.:* донесётся, донесу́тся; донёсся, донесла́сь, донесло́сь, донесли́сь*) be heard*

до́нья *see* дно

^B **допуска́ть** / **допусти́ть** (допущу́, допу́стит, допу́стят)

1) *(*кого́ / что до кого́ / чего́*) admit (smb. / smth. to smb. / smth.)*

2) *permit, allow*

допу́стим, что… = *let us assume that…*

допусти́ть *see* **допуска́ть**

ᴬ **доро́га** *road*

уста́ть с доро́ги = *be tired after the journey*

туда́ ему́ и доро́га = *that serves him well*

ᴬ **дорого́й** (до́рог, дорога́, до́рого; доро́же)

1) *expensive*

2) *dear*

доро́же *see* **дорого́й**

ᴮ **доро́жка** *(gen. pl.* доро́жек*)*

1) *path, walk*

2) *strip of carpet, stair-carpet, runner*

ᴮ **доса́да** *vexation, annoyance*

ᴮ **доска́** *(sg. acc.* до́ску, *gen.* доски́, *pl. nom.* до́ски, *gen.* досо́к, *dat.* доска́м*)*

1) *board, plank*

2) *blackboard*

ᴬ **достава́ть** (достаю́, достаёт, достаю́т) / **доста́ть** (доста́ну, доста́нет, доста́нут)

1) *take, get, obtain*

2) (до чего́) *reach (smth.)*

доста́вить *see* **доставля́ть**

ᶜ **доставля́ть** / **доста́вить** (доста́влю, доста́вит, доста́вят)

1) *supply*

2) *convey*

3) *cause, give, afford*

ᴮ **доста́точно** *enough, sufficiently*

доста́ть *see* **достава́ть**

ᶜ **достига́ть** / **дости́гнуть** *or* **дости́чь** (дости́гну, дости́гнет, дости́гнут; дости́г, дости́гла, дости́гло, дости́гли)

(чего́) 1) *reach (smth.)*

2) *achieve (smth.)*

дости́гнуть *see* **достига́ть**

дости́чь *see* **достига́ть**

ᴮ **досто́йный** (досто́ин, досто́йна)

(чего́) *worthy (of smth.), deserving (smth.)*

ᶜ **досту́пный** (досту́пен, досту́пна)

1) *accessible, easy of access*
2) *available, within reach*
3) *reasonable*
4) *easily understood*
5) *approachable, affable*

^в **доходи́ть** (дохожу́, дохо́дит, дохо́дят) / **дойти́** (дойду́, дойдёт, дойду́т; дошёл, дошла́, дошло́, дошли́)
(до кого́ / чего́) *reach (smb. | smth.) (on foot)*

^в **до́чка** *(gen. pl. до́чек) daughter*

^А **дочь** *(sg. gen., dat., the prepositional case* до́чери, *instr.* до́черью, *pl. nom.* до́чери, *gen.* дочере́й, *dat.* дочеря́м, *instr.* дочерьми́, *the prepositional case* дочеря́х) *daughter*

^с **драгоце́нный** (драгоце́нен, драгоце́нна)
1) *precious*
2) *dear*

^с **дразни́ть** (дразню́, дра́знит, дра́знят) *(ipf.) tease*

^в **дра́ться** (деру́сь, дерётся, деру́тся; дра́лся, драла́сь, драло́сь, дра́ли́сь) *(ipf.)*
1) (с кем / чем) *fight (with smb. | smth.)*
2) (за что) *fight (for smth.)*

^в **дре́вний** (дре́вен, дре́вня) *ancient, antique*

^с **дрема́ть** (дремлю́, дре́млет, дре́млют) *(ipf.) doze, slumber*

^в **дрова́** *(n., only pl.) firewood*

дро́гнуть *see* **дрожа́ть**

^в **дрожа́ть** (дрожу́, дрожи́т, дрожа́т) / **дро́гнуть** (дро́гну, дро́гнет, дро́гнут) *shiver, tremble, shake*

^А **друг** *(pl. nom.* друзья́, *gen.* друзе́й) *friend*

^А **друг дру́га** *each other, one another*

^А **друго́й** *other, another, different*
на друго́й день = *the next day*

^А **дру́жба** *friendship*

^в **дружи́ть** (дружу́, дру́жи́т, дру́жа́т) *(ipf.)*
(с кем) *be friends (with smb.)*

^A **дру́жный** (дру́жен, дружна́, дру́жно) *friendly, unanimous, harmonious*

^C **дуб** *(pl. E)*
    1) *oak*
    2) *(dry) stick*

^A **ду́мать, по-** *think, consider, reflect*

^C **ду́ра** *fool (ab. woman)*

^B **дура́к** *(E) fool*

^B **дурно́й** (ду́рён, дурна́, ду́рно, ду́рны́)
    1) *bad*
    2) *evil*

^B **дуть** (ду́ю, ду́ет, ду́ют) *(ipf.) blow*

^B **дух** *(gen. ду́ха / ду́ху) spirit*
    собра́ться с ду́хом = *take heart*
    пасть ду́хом = *lose courage*

^A **душа́** *(sg. acc. ду́шу, gen. души́, pl. ду́ши) soul*
    душа́ моя́! = *my dear!*
    э́то мне по душе́ = *I like it*

^B **душе́вный**
    1) *psychic, mental*
    2) *sincere, cordial*

^C **ду́шный** (ду́шен, душна́, ду́шно) *close, stuffy*

^B **дым** (в дыму́; *pl.* дымы́) *smoke*

^C **дыра́** *(pl. ды́ры)*
    1) *hole*
    2) *god-forsaken hole*

^B **дыха́ние** *breathing, respiration*

^B **дыша́ть** (дышу́, ды́шит, ды́шат) (ipf.) *breathe*

^A **дя́дя** *(gen. pl. дя́дей) uncle*

Е

^A **его́**
    1) *see* **он** *and* **оно́**
    2) *his, its, of it*

^C **еда́** *food*

^A **едва́**
    1) *hardly, only just*

2) *hardly (... when), no sooner (... than)*
едва́ ли не = *almost*
^A еди́нственный *only, sole*
^B еди́ный *united, common*
все до еди́ного = *to a man*
^A её
1) *see* она́
2) *her, hers, its, of it*
^A е́здить (е́зжу, е́здит е́здят) *(indet. vb. of motion)*
(ipf.) drive, ride, go, travel
ей *see* она́
^B ей-бо́гу *really (and truly), I swear*
^B е́ле *hardly, only just*
^B ёлка *(gen. pl. ёлок) fir-tree, spruce, Christmas tree*
ему́ *see* он *and* оно́
^A е́сли *if*
^A есте́ственный *natural*
есть *see* быть
^A есть (ем, ешь, ест, еди́м, еди́те, едя́т; ешь), съ-
eat
^A е́хать (е́ду, е́дет, е́дут) *(det. vb. of motion) (ipf.)*
drive, ride, go, travel
^A ещё *still, yet; some more*
ещё бы! = *I should think so! of course!*
е́ю *see* она́

Ж

ж *see* же
^B жа́дный (жа́ден, жадна́, жа́дно, жа́дны́)
1) *greedy*
2) *covetous*
3) *stingy*
^B жале́ть (жале́ю, жале́ет, жале́ют), по-
1) (кого́) *pity (smb.)*
2) (о чём *or* чего́) *be sorry (for smth.), regret
(smth.)*
3) не жале́ть чего́ *spare nothing*

^в **жа́лкий** (жа́лок, жалка́, жа́лко; жа́льче) *pitiful, poor, wretched*

^А **жа́лко** (жаль)
    1) (кого́ / что, *the subject in dat.*) *pity (smb. / smth.)*
    2) *(followed by the conjunction* что*) it is a pity that*
    мне жаль его́ = *I am sorry for him*

^в **жа́ловаться** (жа́луюсь, жа́луется, жа́луются), **по-**
    (на кого́ / что) *complain (of smb. / smth.)*

    жаль *see* **жа́лко**

    жа́льче *see* **жа́лкий**

^в **жар** *heat, ardour*

^с **жа́рить** (жа́рю, жа́рит, жа́рят), **за-, из-**
    1) *fry, roast*
    2) *burn (ab. the sun)*

^в **жа́ркий** (жа́рок, жарка́, жа́рко; жа́рче) *hot*
    жа́рче *see* **жа́ркий**

^А **ждать** (жду, ждёт, ждут; ждал, ждала́, жда́ло, жда́ли)
    1) (кого́ / что *or* кого́ / чего́) *wait (for smb. / smth.), expect (smb. / smth.)*
    2) (чего́) *expect (smth.)*

^А **же** (ж)
    1) *and, as for, but*
    2) *after all*
    мы уезжа́ем, Ива́н же остаётся = *we are leaving, but Ivan is staying*
    Почему́ вы ему́ не ве́рите? Он же врач = *Why don't you trust him? After all, he's a doctor*

^А **жела́ть, по-**
    (кому́ / чему́ чего́ *or inf.*) *wish (smb. / smth. smth. or that...)*

^в **желе́зный** *iron, ferrous*
    желе́зная доро́га = *railway*

^с **желе́зо** *iron*

^А **жёлтый** (жёлт, желта́, жёлто́, жёлты) *yellow*

^A **жена́** *(pl. жёны)* *wife*

^C **жена́тый** *married (ab. the husband)*

^B **жени́ться** (женю́сь, же́нится, же́нятся) *(ipf. / pf.)*
(на ком) *marry (smb.) (ab. the marriage of a man)*

^C **жени́х** *(gen.* жениха́*) fiancé, betrothed*

^B **же́нский**
1) *female, womanlike*
2) *feminine (grammar)*

^A **же́нщина** *woman*
же́нщина-врач = *woman doctor*

^C **же́ртва**
1) *sacrifice, offering*
2) *victim*

^B **жест** *gesture*

^C **жёсткий** (жёсток, жестка́, жёстко; жёстче) *hard, rigid, stiff*

^B **жесто́кий** (жесто́к, жестока́, жесто́ко) *cruel, brutal, severe*

жёстче *see* **жёсткий**

^A **живо́й** (жив, жива́, жи́во)
1) *living, live, alive*
2) *lively*

^B **живо́тное** *(adjective used substantively) animal*

^C **жи́зненный**
1) *life, for life, of life*
2) *life-like*
3) *vital*

^A **жизнь** *(f.) life*

^C **жило́й**
1) *dwelling*
2) *inhabited, fit to live in*

^B **жи́тель** *(m.) inhabitant, resident, dweller*

^A **жить** (живу́, живёт, живу́т; жил, жила́, жи́ло, жи́ли (не́ жил, не жила́, не́ жило, не́ жили)) *(ipf.) live*
жил-был = *(once upon a time) there was*

^B **журна́л** *periodical, journal*

3

A **за** *(prep. + acc. or instr.)*
  (+ acc.)
   1) *behind, out of*
   2) *by*
   3) *for*
   4) *(in return) for*
   5) за … до *before*
   6) *in*
   7) *(indicating time or measure) above*
  (+ instr.)
   1) *behind, beyond*
   2) *after*
   3) *for*
   4) *at*
   стать за дéрево = *take one's stand behind a tree*
   брóсить чтó-нибудь за окнó = *throw something out of the window*
   взять когó-нибудь зá руку = *take somebody by the hand*
   борóться за свобóду = *fight for freedom*
   платить за книги = *pay for the books*
   за пять дней до срóка = *five days before the term*
   дéлать рабóту за недéлю = *do the work in a week*
   емý зá сорок = *he is above forty*
   стоять за дéревом = *stand behind a tree*
   читáть книгу за книгой = *read one book after another*
   послáть за врачóм = *send for the doctor*
   за обéдом = *at dinner*
в **забирáться / забрáться** (заберýсь, заберётся, за-

беру́тся; забра́лся, забрала́сь, забра́лось, забра́ли́сь)

(followed by a prep. indicating direction) perch, get, climb (on, upon)

B **заболева́ть** / **заболе́ть** (заболе́ю, заболе́ет, заболе́ют) *fall ill*

заболе́ть *see* **заболева́ть**

B **забо́р** *fence*

B **забо́та** *anxiety, trouble, care*

B **забо́титься** (забо́чусь, забо́тится, забо́тятся), по-

(о ком / чём) *take care (of smb. / smth.), look after (smb. / smth.)*

C **забо́тливый** *considerate, careful*

забра́ться *see* **забира́ться**

A **забыва́ть** / **забы́ть** (забу́ду, забу́дет, забу́дут) *forget*

забы́ть *see* **забыва́ть**

завести́ *see* **заводи́ть**

B **зави́довать** (зави́дую, зави́дует, зави́дуют), по-

(кому́ / чему́) *envy (smb. / smth.)*

B **зави́сеть** (зави́шу, зави́сит, зави́сят) *(ipf.)*

(от кого́ / чего́) *depend (on smb. / smth.)*

A **заво́д** *works, factory, mill, plant*

C **заводи́ть** (завожу́, заво́дит, заво́дят) / **завести́** (заведу́, заведёт, заведу́т; завёл, завела́, завело́, завели́)

1) *bring (in (on one's way to a place))*

2) *take, lead, too far away*

3) *arrange, settle*

4) *acquire*

5) *start, raise*

6) *wind up*

A **за́втра** *tomorrow*

B **за́втрак**

1) *breakfast*

2) *lunch*

A **за́втракать, по-**

1) *have breakfast*
2) *have lunch*

с **за́втрашний** *tomorrow's, of tomorrow*

завяза́ть *see* **завя́зывать**

в **завя́зывать / завяза́ть** (завяжу́, завя́жет, завя́жут)
1) *tie up*
2) *bandage*
3) *start, set up*

загаси́ть *see* **гаси́ть**

в **загля́дывать / загляну́ть** (загляну́, загля́нет, загля́нут)
(followed by a prep. indicating direction)
1) *peep, glance (in(to), out, under)*
2) *drop in*

загляну́ть *see* **загля́дывать**

с **загора́ться / загоре́ться** (загорю́сь, загори́тся, загоря́тся)
1) *catch fire*
2) *break out*

в **загоре́лый** *sunburnt, tanned*

загоре́ться *see* **загора́ться**

в **зада́ние** *task, job*

а **зада́ча** *task, problem*

в **за́дний** *back, rear*
за́дний план = *background*

заду́маться *see* **заду́мываться**

в **заду́мчивый** *thoughtful, pensive, given to reverie*

в **заду́мываться / заду́маться** *meditate, ponder*

зажа́рить *see* **жа́рить**

заже́чь *see* **зажига́ть**

в **зажига́ть / заже́чь** (зажгу́, зажжёт, зажгу́т; зажёг, зажгла́, зажгло́, зажгли́)
1) *put on fire*
2) *kindle*

зайти́ *see* **заходи́ть**

заказа́ть *see* **зака́зывать**

^C **зака́зывать / заказа́ть** (закажу́, зака́жет, зака́жут) *order*

^A **зака́нчивать / зако́нчить** (зако́нчу, зако́нчит, зако́нчат) *finish, end*

^B **заключа́ть / заключи́ть** (заключу́, заключи́т, заключа́т)

    1) *lock up, shut up, arrest*

    2) *conclude, infer*

    3) *close*

    4) *contract, enter into*

    де́ло заключа́ется в сле́дующем = *the problem is the following*

    заключа́ть в себе́ = *contain*

    заключа́ть в объя́тия = *take in one's arms*

    заключа́ть в ско́бки = *bracket*

заключи́ть *see* **заключа́ть**

^B **зако́н** *law, act, statute*

зако́нчить *see* **зака́нчивать**

^A **закрыва́ть / закры́ть** (закро́ю, закро́ет, закро́ют) *shut, close, cover*

закры́ть *see* **закрыва́ть**

^A **зал** *hall, reception-room*

^C **залива́ть / зали́ть** (залью́, зальёт, залью́т; зале́й; за́лил, залила́, за́лило, за́лили)

    1) *flood, inundate*

    2) (что чем) *pour (smth. over smth.)*

    3) *extinguish (with water)*

зали́ть *see* **залива́ть**

замени́ть *see* **заменя́ть**

^B **заменя́ть / замени́ть** (заменю́, заме́нит, заме́нят)

    1) (кого / что кем / чем) *replace (smb. / smth. by smb. / smth.)*

    2) (кого / что) *take the place (of smb. / smth.)*

замере́ть *see* **замира́ть**

^C **замерза́ть / замёрзнуть** (замёрзну, замёрзнет, замёрзнут; замёрз, замёрзла, замёрзло, замёрзли)

    1) *be frozen, freeze up*

2) *freeze*

замёрзнуть *see* **замерзать**

C **заместитель** *(m.) deputy*

заметить *see* **замечать**

B **заметный** (заметен, заметна)

    1) *noticeable, visible*

    2) *outstanding*

A **замечательный** (замечателен, замечательна)

    remarkable, splendid, outstanding

A **замечать / заметить** (замечу, заметит, заметят)

    1) *notice, observe*

    2) *remark*

C **замирать / замереть** (замру, замрёт, замрут; замер, замерла, замерло, замерли)

    1) *stand (stock-)still, sink (ab. the heart)*

    2) *die away (ab. sound)*

C **замок** *(gen. замка) lock*

C **замужем**

    (за кем) *married (ab. woman) (to smb.)*

    выйти замуж за кого = *marry smb.*

    он выдал дочь замуж за него = *he had his daughter married to him*

замучить *see* **мучить**

C **занавеска** *(gen. pl. занавесок) curtain*

A **занимать / занять** (займу, займёт, займут; занял, заняла, заняло, заняли)

    1) *occupy, take up*

    2) *capture*

    3) *take (a certain time)*

    4) *occupy (by means of troops)*

A **заниматься / заняться** (займусь, займётся, займутся; занялся, занялась, занялось, занялись)

    1) *(only ipf.) study*

    2) (чем) *be occupied (with smth.)*

    3) (с кем) *devote much attention (to smb.)*

B **занятие**

    1) *occupation, pursuit, business*

    2) *(only pl.) studies, lessons*

3) *occupation (by means of troops)*
заня́ть *see* **занима́ть**
заня́ться *see* **занима́ться**
ᵛ **за́пад** *west*
ᵛ **за́пах** *smell, odour*
запере́ть *see* **запира́ть**
ᶜ **запира́ть / запере́ть** (запру́, запрёт, запру́т; за́пер, заперла́, за́перло, за́перли)
   1) *lock*
   2) *(кого́ / что) lock (smb. / smth.) up*
ᵛ **запи́ска** *(gen. pl.* запи́сок)
   1) *note*
   2) *(only pl.) notes, memoirs, transactions*
заплати́ть *see* **плати́ть**
ᵛ **запомина́ть / запо́мнить** (запо́мню, запо́мнит, запо́мнят) *remember, memorize*
запо́мнить *see* **запомина́ть**
запрети́ть *see* **запреща́ть**
ᶜ **запреща́ть / запрети́ть** (запрещу́, запрети́т, запретя́т)
   (кому́ / чему́ что) forbid (smb. / smth. smth.)
ᶜ **запуска́ть / запусти́ть** (запущу́, запу́стит, запу́стят)
   1) *(что) fling (smth.), (чем в кого́ / во что) fling (smth. at smb. / smth.)*
   2) *launch*
   3) *start (motor)*
   4) *thrust*
   5) *neglect*
запусти́ть *see* **запуска́ть**
ᶜ **зара́нее** *beforehand*
заре́зать *see* **ре́зать**
ᶜ **заря́** *(sg. acc.* зарю́ / зо́рю, *gen.* зари́, *pl. nom.* зо́ри *gen.* зорь *dat.* заря́м / зо́рям)
   1) *dawn, evening-glow*
   2) *(acc. sg.* зарю́) *outset, start*
   3) *(acc. sg.* зо́рю, *dat. pl.* зо́рям) *reveille, retreat*
засну́ть *see* **засыпа́ть**

заста́вить *see* **заставля́ть**

A **заставля́ть / заста́вить** (заста́влю, заста́вит, заста́вят) *force, compel, make*

C **застёгивать / застегну́ть** (застегну́, застегнёт, застегну́т) *button up*

застегну́ть *see* **застёгивать**

A **засыпа́ть / засну́ть** (засну́, заснёт, засну́т) *fall asleep*

A **зате́м** *then, thereupon*

зате́м, что́бы = *(in order) to*

C **затиха́ть / зати́хнуть** (зати́хну, зати́хнет, зати́хнут; зати́х, зати́хла, зати́хло, зати́хли) *calm down, die away*

зати́хнуть *see* **затиха́ть**

A **зато́** *(to make up) for it, in return*

захвати́ть *see* **захва́тывать**

C **захва́тывать / захвати́ть** (захвачу́, захва́тит, захва́тят)

1) *take, snatch*
2) *capture*
3) *take (away)*
4) *seize*

A **заходи́ть** (захожу́, захо́дит, захо́дят) / **зайти́** (зайду́, зайдёт, зайду́т; зашёл, зашла́, зашло́, зашли́)

1) (на / во что) *call (at smth.)*
2) (к кому́) *call (on smb.)*
3) (за кем / чем) *(go to) fetch (smb. / smth.)*

зайти́ за́ угол = *turn the corner*
со́лнце зашло́ = *the sun has set*
речь зашла́ о де́тях = *the conversation turned on the children*

A **заче́м** *why*

C **защи́та** *defence, protection, safeguard*

защити́ть *see* **защища́ть**

B **защища́ть / защити́ть** (защищу́, защити́т, защитя́т) *defend*

заяви́ть *see* **заявля́ть**

^В **заявля́ть / заяви́ть** (заявлю́, зая́вит, зая́вят) *declare, announce*

^В **зва́ние** *title, name, rank*

^А **звать** (зову́, зовёт, зову́т; звал, звала́, зва́ло, зва́ли), **по-**
1) *call*
2) *ask, invite*
меня́ зову́т Петро́м = *my name is Peter*

^А **звезда́** *(pl.* звёзды*) star*

^С **звене́ть** *(only in the 3rd pers.:* звени́т, звеня́т*) (ipf.) ring, clink, jingle*

^В **зверь** *(f.) (pl. gen.* звере́й, *dat.* зверя́м, *instr.* зверя́ми / зверьми́*) (wild) beast*

^А **звони́ть** (звоню́, звони́т, звоня́т), **по-** *ring, telephone, clang*

^В **звоно́к** *(gen.* звонка́*)*
1) *bell*
2) *telephone call*

^А **звук** *sound*

^В **звуча́ть** *(only in the 3rd pers.:* звучи́т, звуча́т*) (ipf.) sound, ring, be heard*

^А **зда́ние** *building*

^А **здесь** *here*

^С **здоро́ваться, по-**
(с кем) *greet (smb.)*

^А **здоро́вый** *healthy, strong, robust*
бу́дьте здоро́вы! = *good-bye!*

^В **здоро́вье** *health*
за ва́ше здоро́вье! = *to your health!*
на здоро́вье! = *you are welcome!*

^А **здра́вствовать** (здра́вствую, здра́вствует, здра́вствуют) *(ipf.) be well, prosper, thrive*
здра́вствуй(те)! = *how do you do! good morning! good afternoon! good evening! good day!*
да здра́вствует свобо́да! = *long live the cause of freedom!*

^А **зелёный** (зе́лен, зелена́, зе́лено) *green*

^А **земля́** *(sg. acc.* зе́млю, *gen.* земли́, *pl. nom.* зе́мли,

^{gen.} *gen.* земе́ль, *dat.* зе́млям)

1) *the Earth*
2) *land*
3) *soil*

^в **земно́й**

earthly, terrestrial

кла́няться зе́мно = *make a low bow*

^в **зе́ркало** *(pl.* зеркала́) *looking-glass, mirror*

^с **зерно́** *(pl. nom.* зёрна, *gen.* зёрен)

1) *grain, seed*
2) *corn*

^А **зима́** *(sg. acc.* зи́му, *gen.* зимы́, *pl.* зи́мы) *winter*

зимо́й = *in winter*

^в **зи́мний** *wintry, winter*

злее *see* **злой**

^в **злой** (зол, зла, зло, злы; злее) *wicked, malicious,*
angry

^в **знак** *sign, token, mark*

^А **знако́миться** (знако́млюсь, знако́мится, зна-
ко́мятся), **по-**

(с кем / чем) *make the acquaintance (of smb. /*
smth.)

^с **знако́мство**

1) *acquaintance*
2) *acquaintances*
3) *familiarity*

^А **знако́мый**

1) *familiar, acquainted*
2) *acquaintance*

^в **знамени́тый** *famous*

^с **зна́мя** *(sg. gen., dat., the prepositional case* зна́-
мени, *instr.* зна́менем, *pl. nom.* знамёна, *gen.*
знамён) *banner, colours*

^в **зна́ние**

1) *knowledge*
2) *(only pl.) erudition, accomplishments*

^А **знать** *(ipf.) know*

^в **значе́ние**

1) *significance, meaning, sense*
2) *importance*

^в **значи́тельный** (значи́телен, значи́тельна)
1) *considerable*
2) *significant*
3) *important*

^A **зна́чить** (зна́чу, зна́чит, зна́чат) *(ipf.)* *mean, signify*

зол *see* **злой**

^C **золоти́стый** *golden*

^в **зо́лото** *gold*

^A **золото́й** *gold, golden*

^в **зри́тель** *(m.)* *spectator, onlooker*

^в **зря** *to no purpose, for nothing*

^A **зуб** *(gen. pl.* зубо́в*)*
1) *tooth*
2) *(pl. nom.* зу́бья, *gen.* зу́бьев*)* *tooth, (mill-)cog*

И

^A **и**
1) *and*
2) *too, either*
и ..., и *both ... and, as well ... as*

^C **и́бо** *for*

^в **игра́** *(pl.* и́гры*)*
1) *play*
2) *acting, performance, game*

^A **игра́ть / сыгра́ть**
1) (во что) *play (at smth.)*
2) *(во что)* *play (smth.) (a game),* (на чём) *play (smth.) (the piano, the violin, etc.)*

^в **игру́шка** *(gen. pl.* игру́шек*)* *toy, plaything*

^в **иде́я** *idea (gen. pl.* иде́й*)*

^A **идти́** (иду́, идёт, иду́т; шёл, шла, шло, шли) *(det. vb. of motion) (ipf.)*
1) *go, walk*

2) *(ab. the movement of means of conveyance)*
go, start, leave

дождь идёт = *it is raining*

зелёное пальто́ вам идёт = *the green coat becomes you*

A **из** (и́зо) *(prep. + gen.)*

1) *out of*
2) *from*
3) *of*

и́зо дня в день = *day by day*

B **изба́** *(pl.* и́збы)

1) *(wooden) peasant house*
2) *cottage, hut*

C **избира́ть / избра́ть** (изберу́, изберёт, изберу́т; избра́л, избрала́, избра́ло, избра́ли)

1) *choose*
2) *elect*

избра́ть *see* **избира́ть**

A **изве́стный** (изве́стен, изве́стна)

1) *well-known, famous*
2) *a certain*

извини́ть *see* **извиня́ть**

B **извиня́ть / извини́ть** (извиню́, извини́т, извиня́т)
excuse, pardon

C **изво́зчик**

1) *carrier, cabman*
2) *cab (with a cabman)*

B **и́здали** *from a distance*

изжа́рить *see* **жа́рить**

A **из-за** *(prep. + gen.)*

1) *from behind*
2) *because of*

измени́ть *see* **изменя́ть**

B **изменя́ть / измени́ть** (изменю́, изме́нит, изме́нят)

1) *change*
2) (кому́ / чему́) *betray (smb. / smth.)*

изму́чить *see* **му́чить**

и́зо *see* **из**

---

^A **из-под** *(prep. + gen.)*
  1) *from under*
  2) *from (a place near some other place)*
^C **изумле́ние** *amazement, wonder*
^B **изуча́ть / изучи́ть** (изучу́, изу́чит, изу́чат) *study*
  изучи́ть *see* **изуча́ть**
^A **и́ли** *or*
  и́ли. . . , и́ли = *either. . . or*
  им *see* **он** *and* **оно́** *and* **они́**
^A **и́менно** *just, exactly*
  а и́менно = *namely*
^A **име́ть** (име́ю, име́ет, име́ют) *(ipf.) have*
^B **име́ться** *(only in the 3rd pers.:* име́ется, име́ются)
  (ipf.) be found, exist
  и́ми *see* **они́**
^A **и́мя** *(n.) (gen., dat., the prepositional case* и́мени,
  instr. и́менем, *pl. nom.* имена́, *gen.* имён, *dat.*
  имена́м) *name, Christian name*
  от и́мени Ива́на = *on Ivan's behalf*
  Библиоте́ка и́мени Ле́нина = *The Lenin Library*
^A **и́на́че**
  1) *differently, in a different way*
  2) *or (else)*
  так и́ли и́на́че = *in some way or other, in any
  case*
^A **инжене́р** *engineer*
^A **иногда́** *sometimes*
^B **ино́й**
  1) *(an)other, (a) different*
  2) *some*
^B **иностра́нец** *(gen.* иностра́нца) *foreigner*
^B **иностра́нный** *foreign*
^A **институ́т**
  1) *institute*
  2) *institution*
^B **инструме́нт** *instrument, tool*
^C **интеллиге́нция** *intelligentsia, intellectuals*
^B **интере́с** *interest*

^A **интере́сный** (интере́сен, интере́сна) *interesting*
интере́сно = *I should like to know*

^B **интересова́ться** (интересу́юсь, интересу́ется, интересу́ются) *(ipf.)*
(кем / чем) *be interested (in smb. / smth.)*

и пр. *see* **про́чий**

^C **иро́ния** *irony*

^A **иска́ть** (ищу́, и́щет, и́щут) *(ipf.)*
1) *look for, search for*
2) (что *or* чего́) *seek (smth.)*

^C **исключе́ние**
1) *exclusion, expulsion*
2) *exception*

^C **и́скренний** (и́скренен, и́скренна, и́скренно / и́скренне, и́скренны / и́скренни) *sincere, frank*

искупа́ться *see* **купа́ться**

^C **иску́сственный**
1) *artificial*
2) *affected*

^B **иску́сство**
1) *art*
2) *skill, proficiency, craftsmanship*

испо́лнить *see* **исполня́ть**

^B **исполня́ть / испо́лнить** (испо́лню, испо́лнит, испо́лнят)
1) *carry out, fulfil, execute*
2) *perform, act, play*

^C **испо́льзовать** (испо́льзую, испо́льзует, испо́льзуют) *(ipf. / pf.) utilize, make use of, take advantage of*

испро́бовать *see* **про́бовать**

^B **испу́ганный** *frightened, scared*

испуга́ться *see* **пуга́ться**

испыта́ть *see* **испы́тывать**

^B **испы́тывать / испыта́ть**
1) *try, test*
2) *experience, feel*

^A **исто́рия**

1) *history*
2) *story*
3) *event*

истра́тить *see* **тра́тить**

^A **исчеза́ть/исче́знуть** (исче́зну, исче́знет, исче́знут; исче́з, исче́зла, исче́зло, исче́зли) *disappear, vanish*

исче́знуть *see* **исчеза́ть**

^C **Ита́лия** *Italy*

и т. п. *see* **подо́бный**

^A **их**
1) *see* **они́**
2) *their, theirs*

^A **ию́ль** *(m.) July*

^A **ию́нь** *(m.) June*

К

^A **к** (ко) *(prep. + dat.)*
1) *to, towards*
2) *for*
3) *by*

^C **каба́к** *(in Pre-revolutionary Russia)*
1) *pothouse*
2) *public-house*

^A **кабине́т**
1) *study*
2) *consulting-room*

^A **ка́ждый**
1) *each, every*
2) *everybody, everyone*

^A **каза́ться** (кажу́сь, ка́жется, ка́жутся), **по-**
1) *seem, appear*
2) *(impers.) it seems*

^A **как**
1) *how*
2) *what*
3) *as, like*

как бу́дто = *as if*

как ... так и = *as well ... as*

^B ка́к-нибудь
1) *somehow*
2) *anyhow*
3) *some time*

^A како́й
1) *what*
2) *(such) … as*

^A како́й-нибудь *some*

^A како́й-то *some*

^A ка́к-то
1) *somehow*
2) *somewhat*
3) *one day, once (in the past)*

^B ка́менный
1) *stone, stony*
2) *hard*

^A ка́мень *(gen.* ка́мня, *gen. pl.* камне́й*) stone*

^A кани́кулы *(only pl.) (gen.* кани́кул*) vacation, holidays*

^B капита́н *captain*

^B ка́пля *(gen. pl.* ка́пель*) drop*

^A каранда́ш *(E) pencil*

^A карма́н *pocket*
э́то мне не по карма́ну = *that is more than I can afford*

^B ка́рта
1) *map*
2) *card*

^A карти́на
1) *picture*
2) *scene*

^C карто́фель *(m.) (only sg.) potatoes*

^B каса́ться / косну́ться (косну́сь, коснётся, косну́тся)
(кого́ / чего́) 1) *touch (smb. / smth.)*
2) *concern (smb. / smth.)*

^A ката́ться *(ipf.)*
1) *roll*

2) (на чём) *go along, move along (on smth.)*

катáться на конькáх = *skate, go skating*

катáться на лóдке = *boat, go boating*

^B **катúть** (качý, кáтит, кáтят) *(ipf.)*

1) *roll, wheel*

2) *drive*

^C **качáться / качнýться** (качнýсь, качнётся, качнýтся)

1) *rock, swing*

2) *reel, stagger*

^B **кáчество** *quality*

качнýться *see* качáться

кáшлянуть *see* кáшлять

^C **кáшлять / кáшлянуть** (кáшляну, кáшлянет, кáшлянут) *cough*

^B **квадрáтный** *square*

^A **квартúра** *flat, apartment*

^A **кивáть / кивнýть** (кивнý, кивнёт, кивнýт) *nod*

кивнýть *see* кивáть

^B **килогрáмм** *kilogramme*

^A **киломéтр** *kilometre*

^A **кинó** *(indeclinable n.) cinema*

^C **киóск** *kiosk*

^C **кипéть** (киплю́, кипúт, кипя́т), **вс-** *boil, seethe*

^C **кúслый** (кúсел, кислá, кúсло) *sour, acid*

^C **Китáй** *China*

^B **клáняться / поклонúться** (поклоню́сь, поклóнишься, поклóнятся)

1) (комý / чемý) *bow (to smb. / smth.)* (с кем) *greet (smb.)*

2) (комý / чемý от когó) *give (smb. / smth. smb.'s) best regards*

3) (комý / чемý) *bow and scrape (before smb. / smth.)*

Почемý вы с нúми не клáняетесь? = *Why are you not on speaking terms with them?*

^A **класс** *class*

^A **класть** (кладý, кладёт, кладýт; клал, клáла,

кла́ло, кла́ли) / **положи́ть** (положу́, поло́жит, поло́жат) *lay, put, place*

C **кле́тка** *(gen. pl.* кле́ток*)*
   1) *cage*
   2) *check*
   3) *cell*

A **клуб** *club*

B **ключ** *(E)*
   1) *key, clue*
   2) *source, spring*

A **кни́га** *book*

B **кни́жка** *(gen. pl.* кни́жек*) (small) book*

C **княги́ня** *princess*

C **князь** *(m.) (pl. nom.* князья́, *gen.* князе́й*) prince*
   ко *see* к

C **ковёр** *(gen.* ковра́*) carpet, rug*

A **когда́** *when, as, while*

B **когда́-нибудь** *some time, some day, ever*

B **когда́-то** *once (upon a time), formerly*

B **ко́е-что** *something*

B **ко́жа**
   1) *skin, hide*
   2) *leather*
   3) *peel, rind*

B **колеба́ться** (коле́блюсь, коле́блется, коле́блют-ся), по-
   1) *(only in the 3rd pers.) oscillate, vacillate*
   2) *(only in the 3rd pers.) fluctuate*
   3) *hesitate, waver*

B **коле́но** *(pl. nom.* коле́ни, *gen.* коле́ней, *dat.* коле́ням) knee*

B **колесо́** *(pl.* колёса*) wheel*

B **коли́чество** *quantity, amount, number*

C **коллекти́в** *collective (body), association*

C **коло́дец** *(gen.* коло́дца*) well*

C **коло́нна** *column*

A **колхо́з** *(abbreviation of* коллекти́вное хозя́йство*) kolkhoz (Soviet Russian collective farm)*

66

^B **колхо́зник** *peasant working at a (Soviet Russian) collective farm*

^C **кольцо́** *(pl. nom.* ко́льца, *gen.* коле́ц, *dat.* ко́льцам) *ring*

^B **кома́нда**

1) *command, order*

2) *party, detachment, crew*

^B **команди́р** *commander, captain, commanding officer*

^C **комбина́т** *(Soviet Russian) group of enterprises*

^C **коми́ссия** *commission, committee*

^B **комите́т** *committee*

^B **коммуни́зм** *Communism*

^C **коммуни́ст** *Communist*

^B **коммунисти́ческий** *Communist*

^A **ко́мната** *room*

^A **комсомо́л** *(abbreviation of* (Всесою́зный Ле́нинский) Коммунисти́ческий Сою́з Молодёжи) *Komsomol (Young Communist League)*

^A **конёк** *(gen.* конька́) *skate*

^A **коне́ц** *(gen.* конца́) *end, ending*

в конце́ концо́в = *in the end, after all, ultimately*

своди́ть концы́ с конца́ми = *make both ends meet*

из конца́ в коне́ц = *in all directions*

^A **коне́чно** *of course, certainly, to be sure*

^C **конто́ра** *office, bureau*

^A **конфе́та** *sweets*

^B **конце́рт** *concert*

^A **конча́ть / ко́нчить** (ко́нчу, ко́нчит, ко́нчат) *end, finish*

ко́нчить *see* **конча́ть**

^B **конь** *(m.) (gen.* коня́, *pl. nom.* ко́ни, *gen.* коне́й) *horse*

^B **копе́йка** *(gen. pl.* копе́ек) *copeck (= 1/100 rouble)*

^B **кора́бль** *(gen.* корабля́) *ship, vessel, liner*

^C **ко́рень** *(gen. sg.* ко́рня, *gen. pl.* корне́й) *root*

^C **корзи́на** *basket*

^A **коридо́р** *corridor, passage*

^B **кори́чневый** *brown*

^B **корми́ть** (кормлю́, ко́рмит, ко́рмят), на-, по-, про-
1) *(pf.* на-, по-*) feed, suckle, nurse*
2) *(pf.* про-*) keep, afford a living*

^C **коро́бка** *(gen. pl.* коро́бок*) box*

^C **коро́ва** *cow*

^C **коро́ль** *(gen.* короля́*) king*

^A **коро́ткий** (ко́ро́ток, коротка́, ко́ро́тко́, ко́ро́тки́; коро́че) *short (the predicative forms* коро́ток, коротка́, коротко́, коротки́ *mean: too short)*
мы с ним на коро́ткой ноге́ = *I am on friendly terms with him*

коро́че *see* **коро́ткий**

^C **ко́рпус** *(pl.* корпуса́*)*
1) *corps*
2) *hull*
3) *building*

^C **коса́** *(sg. acc.* ко́су, *gen.* косы́, *pl.* ко́сы*) plait, tress, braid*

^C **космона́вт** *cosmonaut*

косну́ться *see* **каса́ться**

^C **косо́й** (кос, коса́, ко́со)
1) *slanting, skew, oblique*
2) *crooked*
3) *squinting, squint-eyed*

^B **костёр** *(gen.* костра́*) bonfire*

^C **кость** *(f.)* (в кости́; *gen. pl.* косте́й)
1) *bone*
2) *dice*

^A **костю́м** *costume, dress, suit*

^A **кото́рый** *which, who, that*

^B **ко́фе** *(indeclinable m.) coffee*

^C **ко́шка** *(gen. pl.* ко́шек*) cat*

^A **край** (на краю́; *pl.* края́)
1) *edge, brim, brink*
2) *(в краю́) land, territory*

^B **кра́йний** *extreme, the last*

по кра́йней ме́ре = at least

ᴮ **краса́вица** *(a) beauty*

ᴬ **краси́вый** *beautiful, handsome*

ᶜ **кра́сить** (кра́шу, кра́сит, кра́сят), **вы́-, о-, по-**
paint, colour

ᴮ **кра́ска** *(gen. pl.* кра́сок*)*
1) *paint*
2) *colour*

ᴮ **красне́ть** (красне́ю, красне́ет, красне́ют), **по-**
turn red

ᴬ **кра́сный** (кра́сен, красна́, кра́сно) *red*

ᴮ **красота́** *(pl.* красо́ты*)*
1) *beauty*
2) *(only pl.) (the) charms (of nature)*

ᶜ **красть** (краду́, крадёт, краду́т; крал, кра́ла,
кра́ло, кра́ли), **у-** *steal*

ᴮ **кра́ткий** (кра́ток, кратка́, кра́тко; кра́тче) *short,
brief*

кра́тче *see* **кра́ткий**

ᴬ **кре́пкий** (кре́пок, крепка́, кре́пко; кре́пче) *strong,
firm, vigorous*

ᶜ **крепостно́й** крепостно́е пра́во *serfdom*

ᶜ **кре́пость** *(f.) (gen. pl.* крепосте́й*)*
1) *stronghold*
2) *fortress*

кре́пче *see* **кре́пкий**

ᴮ **кре́сло** *(gen. pl.* кре́сел*) arm-chair, easy-chair,
stall*

ᴮ **крестья́нин** *(pl. nom.* крестья́не, *gen.* крестья́н*)
peasant*

ᶜ **крестья́нка** *(gen. pl.* крестья́нок*)*
1) *peasant woman*
2) *farmer's wife*

ᶜ **криво́й** (крив, крива́, кри́во)
1) *crooked, curved*
2) *false*
3) *one-eyed, blind in one eye*

ᴮ **крик** *(gen.* кри́ка / кри́ку*) cry, shout*

кри́кнуть *see* крича́ть

A **крича́ть** (кричу́, кричи́т, крича́т) / **кри́кнуть** (кри́кну, кри́кнет, кри́кнут) *cry, shout*

A **крова́ть** *(f.) bedstead, bed*

B **кровь** *(f.)* (в крови́) *blood*

A **кро́ме** *(prep. + gen.)*
1) *except*
2) *besides*

B **круг** *(pl. E)*
1) (в, на, кру́ге) *(mathematical) circle*
2) (в кру́ге / в кругу́) *sphere, circle (in society)*

B **кру́глый** (кругл, кругла́, кру́гло) *round*
кру́глый год = *all the year round*
кру́глый сирота́ = *orphan*
кру́глый дура́к = *a perfect fool, an utter fool*

A **круго́м**
1) *(adv.) round, around, all round*
2) *(prep. + gen.) round*

B **кружи́ться** (кружу́сь, кру́жится, кру́жатся) *(ipf.)*
whirl, go round

B **кружо́к** *(gen. кружка́)*
1) *small circle*
2) *circle, hobby group*

B **кру́пный** (кру́пен, крупна́, кру́пно)
1) *large, big*
2) *great, important*
3) *prominent*

C **круто́й** (крут, крута́, кру́то; кру́че)
1) *steep*
2) *sudden, abrupt*

кру́че *see* круто́й

B **крыло́** *(pl. nom.* кры́лья, *gen.* кры́льев*)*
1) *wing (of a bird)*
2) *wing (of a house)*

B **крыльцо́** *(pl. nom.* кры́льца, *gen.* крыле́ц*) porch*

A **кры́ша** *roof*

C **кры́шка** *(gen. pl.* кры́шек*) lid, cover*

B **кста́ти**

1) *to the point, opportunely*
2) *at the same time, incidentally*
3) *by the way, by the by*

^A **кто** *(acc., gen.* кого́, *dat.* кому́, *instr.* кем, *the prepositional case* о ком*) who, that*
кто ..., кто = *one ... the other*

^A **кто́-нибудь** *(as for the declination, see* кто*) somebody, someone, anybody, anyone*

^A **кто́-то** *(as for the declination, see* кто*) somebody*

^A **куда́** *where*
э́то куда́ лу́чше = *that is much better*

^C **куда́-нибудь** *somewhere, anywhere*

^B **куда́-то** *somewhere, anywhere*

^A **ку́кла** *(gen. pl.* ку́кол*) doll*

^B **кула́к** *(E)*
1) *fist*
2) *kulak, rich farmer*

^B **культу́ра** *culture*

^A **купа́ться, вы́-, ис-** *bathe, take a bath*

^B **купе́ц** *(gen.* купца́*) merchant*

купи́ть *see* **покупа́ть**

^B **кури́ть** *(*курю́, ку́рит, ку́рят*) (ipf.) smoke*

^B **курс**
1) *course*
2) *year of study*

^A **ку́ртка** *(gen. pl.* ку́рток*) jacket*

^C **куса́ть / кусну́ть** *(*кусну́, кусне́т, кусну́т*)*
1) *bite*
2) *(only ipf.) sting*

кусну́ть *see* **куса́ть**

^A **кусо́к** *(gen.* куска́*) piece, bit, lump, slice*

^B **кусо́чек** *(gen.* кусо́чка*) small piece, small lump*

^B **куст** *(E) bush, shrub*

^A **ку́хня** *(gen. pl.* ку́хонь*) kitchen*

^B **ку́ча** *heap*

^C **ку́шать, по-, с-** *have, take (food)*

Л

^C лаборато́рия *laboratory*

^B ла́вка *(gen. pl.* ла́вок*)*
   1) *bench*
   2) *small shop*

^B ла́герь *(pl.* лагеря́*) camp*

^A ла́дно *well, all right*

^B ладо́нь *(f.) palm*

^A ла́мпа *lamp*

^C ла́па *paw*

^A ла́сковый *affectionate, tender, sweet*

^C ла́ять (ла́ю, ла́ет, ла́ют) *(ipf.) bark*

^A ле́вый *left, left-hand*

^A лёгкий (лёгок, легка́, легко́, лёгки́; ле́гче)
   1) *light*
   2) *easy*

ле́гче *see* лёгкий

^B лёд *(gen.* льда; на льду*) ice*

^B ледяно́й *icy, glacial*

^A лежа́ть (лежу́, лежи́т, лежа́т) *(ipf.) lie*

^A лезть (ле́зу, ле́зет, ле́зут; лез, ле́зла, ле́зло, ле́зли) *(ipf.) climb, clamber, get*
   лезть в карма́н = *put one's hand in one's pocket, reach into one's pocket*
   сапо́г не ле́зет на́ ногу = *the boot does not fit*

^C лека́рство *medicine*

^B ле́кция *lecture*

^C лени́вый *lazy*

^B ле́нта
   1) *ribbon*
   2) *tape, band*

^A лес (в лесу́; *pl.* леса́) *wood, forest*

^A ле́стница *stairs, staircase*

^A лет *(gen. pl. of* ле́то; лет *is used after numerals above* четы́ре, *after composite numbers ending in numerals above* четы́ре, *and after adverbs indicating quantity; see* год*) years*

^B лета́ть *(indet. vb. of motion) (ipf.) fly*

^A **лете́ть** (лечу́, лети́т, летя́т) *(det. vb. of motion)*
  (ipf.) fly
^B **ле́тний**
  1) *summer*
  2) *summerly*
^A **ле́то** *summer*
  ле́том = *in summer*
^B **лётчик** *pilot, aviator*
^C **лечи́ть** (лечу́, ле́чит, ле́чат) *(ipf.) treat (medically)*
  лечь *see* **ложи́ться**
^A **ли** (ль)
  1) *whether, if*
  2) *not translated*
  вряд ли = *scarcely, hardly*
^C **лимона́д** *lemon squash*
^B **ли́ния** *line*
^A **лист** *(E)*
  1) *leaf (of paper), sheet (of paper)*
  2) *(pl. nom.* ли́стья, *gen.* ли́стьев*) leaf, blade*
^B **литерату́ра** *literature*
^C **лить** (лью, льёт, льют; лей; лил, лила́, ли́ло,
  ли́ли) *(ipf.) pour*
^B **лифт** *lift*
^A **лицо́** *(pl.* ли́ца*)*
  1) *face*
  2) *person*
  пла́тье ей к лицу́ = *the dress suits her*
^A **ли́чный** *personal, private*
^B **ли́шний**
  1) *spare*
  2) *superfluous*
  три киломе́тра с ли́шним = *more than three
    kilometres*
^A **лишь** *only*
^A **лоб** *(gen.* лба; во, на, лбу*) forehead*
^A **лови́ть** (ловлю́, ло́вит, ло́вят) / **пойма́ть** *catch*
^B **ло́вкий** (ло́вок, ловка́, ло́вко; ло́вче) *adroit,
  dexterous, dodgy*

ло́вче *see* ло́вкий

B ло́дка *(gen. plur.* ло́док*) boat*

A ложи́ться (ложу́сь, ложи́тся, ложа́тся) / лечь
(ля́гу, ля́жет, ля́гут; лёг, легла́, легло́, легли́)
lie down

C ло́жка *(gen. pl.* ло́жек*) spoon*

B ло́коть *(m.) (gen. pl.* локте́й*)*
1) *elbow*
2) *old measure, approximately = 0,5 m*
чу́вство ло́ктя = *feeling of fellowship*

C лома́ть, по-, с-
1) *(pf.* по-, с-*) break*
2) *(pf.* с-*) break down, break with*

A ло́шадь *(f.) (pl. gen.* лошаде́й, *instr.* лошадьми́ /
лошадя́ми*) horse*

C лу́жа *puddle, pool*

B луна́ *(pl.* лу́ны*) moon*

B луч *(E) ray, beam*

лу́чше *see* хоро́ший

A лу́чший *best*

A лы́жа *ski*

ль *see* ли

C любе́зный (любе́зен, любе́зна) *amiable, polite,*
obliging

A люби́мый
1) *dear, beloved*
2) *favourite*

A люби́ть (люблю́, лю́бит, лю́бят) *(ipf.)*
1) *love*
2) *like*

C любова́ться (любу́юсь, любу́ется, любу́ются),
по-
(кем / чем) *admire (smb. / smth.), feast one's*
eyes (upon smb. / smth.)

B любо́вь *(f.) (sg. gen.* любви́, *instr.* любо́вью*)*
love

A любо́й *any*

C любопы́тный (любопы́тен, любопы́тна)

1) *curious*
2) *interesting*

^B **любопы́тство** *curiosity*

^A **лю́ди** *(only pl.; gen.* людéй, *dat.* лю́дям, *instr.* людьми́, *the prepositional case* лю́дях) *(used as pl. of* человéк) *people*

М

^A **магази́н** *shop, store*

^A **май** *May*

^A **ма́ленький** *(for predicative forms see* ма́лый; мéньше) *small, little*

^A **ма́ло** (мéньше *or* мéнее) *little, few*
мало-пома́лу = *little by little, gradually*
ма́ло ли что мóжет случи́ться! = *goodness knows what may happen!*

^A **ма́лый** (мал, мала́; мéньше)
1) *small, little*
2) *(only the predicative forms) too small, too little*

^A **ма́льчик** *boy, lad*

^B **мальчи́шка** *(gen. pl.* мальчи́шек) *(small) boy, urchin*

^A **ма́ма** *mummy, mamma*

^A **март** *March*

^B **ма́сло** *(pl. nom.* масла́, *gen.* ма́сел, *dat.* масла́м)
1) *oil*
2) *butter*
3) *oils (painting)*

^C **ма́сса** *mass*

^A **ма́стер** *(pl.* мастера́)
1) *master, expert*
2) *foreman*
ма́стер на все ру́ки = *jack-of-all-trades*

^B **мастерска́я** *(adj. used substantively)*
1) *workshop*
2) *studio*

^C **матема́тика** *mathematics*

^B **материа́л**
1) *material, stuff*
2) *fabric*

^A **матро́с** *seaman, sailor*

^B **мать** *(sg. gen., dat., the prepositional case* ма́тери, *instr.* ма́терью, *pl. nom.* ма́тери, *gen.* матере́й, *dat.* матеря́м) mother*

^B **маха́ть / махну́ть** (махну́, махнёт, махну́т)
1) (чем кому́) *wave ((with) smth. to smb.)*
2) (чем) *flap (smth.) (one's wings)*

махну́ть *see* **маха́ть**

^A **маши́на**
1) *machine, engine*
2) *car*

^C **ме́бель** *(f.) (only sg.) furniture*

^B **медве́дь** *(m.) bear*

^A **ме́дленный** *slow*

^A **ме́жду** *(prep. + instr.)*
1) *between*
2) *among, amongst*
ме́жду про́чим = *by the way*
ме́жду на́ми = *between ourselves*
ме́жду тем, как = *while, whereas*

^B **междунаро́дный** *international*

^A **ме́лкий** (ме́лок, мелка́, ме́лко; ме́льче)
1) *fine*
2) *small*
3) *inconsiderable*
4) *shallow*
5) *flat, ordinary (ab. plate)*

^B **ме́лочь** *(f.) (gen. pl.* мелоче́й)
1) *smallwares*
2) *change*
3) *trifle*

^B **мелька́ть / мелькну́ть** (мелькну́, мелькнёт, мелькну́т) *flash, gleam, appear for a moment*
у него́ мелькну́ла мысль = *an idea flashed across his mind*

мелькну́ть *see* **мелька́ть**

ме́льче *see* **ме́лкий**

ме́нее *see* **ма́ло**

ме́ньше *see* **ма́ленький, ма́ло** *and* **ма́лый**

меня́ *see* **я**

ᴮ **меня́ться, по-**
    1) (чем с кем / чем) *exchange (smth. with smb. / smth.)*
    2) *(only ipf.) take turns*
    3) *(only ipf.) change*

ᴮ **ме́ра**
    1) *measure*
    2) *(only pl.) measures, precautions*
    по ме́ре того́, как ... = *as*

ᴮ **мёртвый** (мёртв, мертва́, мёртво́, мёртвы́)
    1) *dead*
    2) *lifeless*

ᶜ **ме́стность** *(f.) locality, district, country*

ᴬ **ме́сто** *(pl.* места́*)*
    1) *place, spot*
    2) *seat (in theatre)*
    3) *space, room*
    4) *post, office*
    места́ми = *here and there*

ᴬ **ме́сяц**
    1) *month*
    2) *moon*

ᴬ **мета́лл** *metal*

ᶜ **мете́ль** *(f.) snow-storm, blizzard*

ᴮ **метр** *metre*

ᴮ **метро́** *(indeclinable n.) metro, underground*

ᶜ **мех** (на меху́; *pl.* меха́) *fur*

ᶜ **механиза́ция** *mechanization*

ᴮ **меха́ник**
    1) *mechanic*
    2) *mechanical engineer, scientist studying mechanics*

ᶜ **меховой** *fur*

^B **мечта́** *(мечта́ний is used as gen. pl.) dream, day-
dream(ing)*

^A **мечта́ть** *(ipf.) dream*

^A **меша́ть, по-, с-**
1) (кому́ / чему́ + *inf.*) *(pf.* по-*) prevent (smb. /
smth. from (doing))*
2) *(pf.* по-*) stir*
3) *(pf.* с-*) mix*
4) (кому́ / чему́) *(pf.* с-*) disturb (smb. / smth.)*

^B **мешо́к** *(gen.* мешка́*) bag, sack*

^A **милиционе́р** *policeman*

^B **миллио́н** *million*

^A **ми́лый** (мил, мила́, ми́ло, ми́лы) *dear, nice, sweet*

^A **ми́мо** *(adv. and prep. + gen.) past*

^A **мину́та** *minute*

^A **мир**
1) *world*
2) *mir (village community in Pre-revolutionary
Russia)*
3) *peace*

^B **ми́рный** (ми́рен, ми́рна)
1) *peace*
2) *peaceful, peaceable*
3) *quiet*

^C **мирово́й** *world*

^B **мла́дший**
1) *younger, junior*
2) *youngest*

мне *see* **я**

^B **мне́ние** *opinion*

^B **мно́гие** *many, many people*

^A **мно́го** *much*

^B **мно́жество** *great number*

мной *see* **я**

мно́ю *see* **я**

^C **моги́ла** *grave*

^C **могу́чий** *mighty*

^A **мо́жно**

1) *one can*

2) *one may*

мо́жно (мне) взять кни́гу? = *may I take the book?*

как мо́жно скоре́е = *as soon as possible*

^A мой *(gen.* моего́; *f.* моя́, *gen.* мое́й; *n.* моё, *gen.* моего́; *pl.* мои́, *gen.* мои́х) *my, mine*

по-мо́ему

1) *in my opinion*

2) *as I want, as I would have it*

^A мо́крый (мокр, мокра́, мо́кро) *wet, moist*

^B мол *he (she, it) says, they say*

^A молодёжь *(f.) youth, young people*

^B молоде́ц *(gen.* молодца́) *fine boy, fine girl, dab*

^A молодо́й (мо́лод, молода́, мо́лодо; моло́же) *young*

^B мо́лодость *(f.) youth*

моло́же *see* молодо́й

^A молоко́ *milk*

^A мо́лча *silently, tacitly*

^C молчали́вый *taciturn, silent, uncommunicative*

^A молча́ть (молчу́, молчи́т, молча́т) *(ipf.) keep silent*

^B моме́нт

1) *moment, instant*

2) *feature, point*

^A мо́ре *(pl. E, gen. pl.* море́й) *sea*

^A моро́женое *(adj. used substantively) ice-cream*

^A моро́з *frost*

^B морско́й *sea, maritime, marine*

^C морщи́нка *(gen. pl.* морщи́нок)

1) *little crease*

2) *wrinkle*

^B моря́к *(gen.* моряка́) *sailor*

^B моско́вский *Moscow*

^B мост (мо́ста́; на мосту́; *pl. E) bridge*

^C мото́р *motor, engine*

^A мочь (могу́, мо́жет, мо́гут; мог, могла́, могло́,

могли́), **с-** *be able*

мо́жет быть = *perhaps*

^В **мо́щный** (мо́щен, мощна́, мо́щно)
1) *strong, powerful, forceful*
2) *huge, enormous*

^В **мра́чный** (мра́чен, мрачна́)
1) *gloomy, sombre, dark*
2) *dismal, dreary*

^А **муж** *(pl. nom.* мужья́, *gen.* муже́й, *dat.* мужья́м)
husband

^С **му́жество** *courage*

^С **мужи́к** *(E) muzhik, peasant (in Pre-revolutionary Russia)*

^С **мужско́й** *men's, gentlemen's, male, masculine*

^В **мужчи́на** *man, male*

^А **музе́й** *museum*

^А **му́зыка** *music*

^С **му́чить** (му́чу, му́чит, му́чат), **за-, из-** *torment, harass, worry, trouble*

^В **мча́ться** (мчусь, мчи́тся, мча́тся) *(ipf.) rush along, tear along, gallop*

^А **мы** *(acc., gen., the prepositional case* нас, *dat.* нам, *instr.* на́ми) *we*

^А **мысль** *(f.) thought, reflection, idea*

^С **мыть** (мо́ю, мо́ет, мо́ют), **вы́-, по-** *wash*

^А **мя́гкий** (мя́гок, мягка́, мя́гко; мя́гче)
1) *soft*
2) *mild, gentle*

мя́гче *see* **мя́гкий**

^В **мя́со** *meat, flesh*

^А **мяч** *(E) ball*

Н

^А **на** *(prep.* + *acc. or the prepositional case)*
(+ *acc.)*
1) *on, on to*
2) *to, for*

3) *(with reference to some means of conveyance)*
   on
4) *for*
5) *(indicating time) on*
6) *(indicating space of time) for*
7) *(in connection with comparative forms, indicating price or measure) not translated*
(+ the prepositional case)
1) *on, in, at*
2) *(with reference to some means of conveyance) by*
3) *(indicating time) during; (indicating year) in; (indicating week) not translated (indicating day) on; not translated*

положи́ть кни́гу на стол = *put the book on the table*

идти́ на рабо́ту = *go to work*

сесть на авто́бус = *get on the bus*

по кни́ге на ка́ждого студе́нта = *a book for each student*

на второ́й день = *on the second day*

он уе́хал на пять дней = *he left for five days*

она́ ста́рше меня́ на́ два го́да = *she is two years older than I*

кни́га лежи́т на столе́ = *the book is on the table*

е́хать на авто́бусе = *go by bus*

на деся́том году́ (свое́й жи́зни) = *in one's tenth year*

на э́той неде́ле = *this week*

на пра́здниках = *on holidays*

^C **набира́ть / набра́ть** (наберу́, наберёт, наберу́т; набра́л, набрала́, набра́ло, набра́ли)
1) *gather*
2) *recruit*
3) *compose*
набра́ть но́мер = *dial a number*
набра́ть ско́рость = *pick up speed*

^в **наблюда́ть** *(ipf.)*
1) *observe*
2) (за кем / чем) *watch (smb. / smth.), supervise (smb. / smth.)*

набра́ть *see* **набира́ть**

^А **наве́рно** (наве́рное) *probably, most likely*

наве́рное *see* **наве́рно**

^С **наве́рх** *up(ward), upstairs, on top*

^С **наверху́** *above, upstairs*

навести́ть *see* **навеща́ть**

^С **навеща́ть / навести́ть** (навещу́, навести́т, навестя́т) *visit, call on*

навра́ть *see* **врать**

^в **навсегда́** *for ever, for good*

^в **навстре́чу** *(adv. and prep. + dat.) to meet*

нагре́ть *see* **греть**

^А **над** (на́до) *(prep. + instr.)*
1) *over, above*
2) *at*

^А **надева́ть / наде́ть** (наде́ну, наде́нет, наде́нут)
1) (что) *put on (smth.)*
2) (что на кого) *put (smth. on smb.)*

^в **наде́жда** *hope*

наде́ть *see* **надева́ть**

^А **наде́яться** (наде́юсь, наде́ется, наде́ются) *(ipf.)*
1) (на что) *hope (for smth.)*
2) (на кого / что) *rely (on smb. / smth.)*

на́до *see* **над**

^А **на́до** *it is necessary, one must, one should, one ought to*
мне на́до уе́хать = *I have to go away*

^в **надоеда́ть / надое́сть** (надое́м, надое́шь, надое́ст, надоеди́м, надоеди́те, надоедя́т)
(кому́ / чему́ чем) *bore (smb. / smth. with smth.), pester (smb. / smth. with smth.)*

надое́сть *see* **надоеда́ть**

^А **наза́д** *back, backwards*
два го́да (тому́) наза́д = *two years ago*

^в **назва́ние** *name, appellation*
назва́ть *see* **называ́ть**
^с **назнача́ть / назна́чить** (назна́чу, назна́чит, назна́чат)
    1) *fix, set, prescribe*
    2) (кого́ кем) *engage (smb. as smth.)*, (кого́ во что) *appoint (smb. to an office)*
назна́чить *see* **назнача́ть**
^А **называ́ть / назва́ть** (назову́, назовёт, назову́т; назва́л, назвала́, назва́ло, назва́ли)
    1) (кого́ / что кем / чем) *call (smb. / smth. smb. / smth.)*
    2) *name*
    3) *(only pf.) invite*
^с **наибо́лее** *most*
^с **наизу́сть** *by heart*
найти́ *see* **находи́ть**
найти́сь *see* **находи́ться**
наказа́ть *see* **нака́зывать**
^с **нака́зывать / наказа́ть** (накажу́, нака́жет, нака́жут) *punish*
^с **накану́не**
    1) *(adv.) the day before*
    2) *(prep. + gen.) on the eve of*
наклони́ть *see* **наклоня́ть**
^в **наклоня́ть / наклони́ть** (наклоню́, накло́нит, накло́нят) *incline, bend*
^А **наконе́ц** *at last*
накорми́ть *see* **корми́ть**
^в **накрыва́ть / накры́ть** (накро́ю, накро́ет, накро́ют)
    (что чем) *cover (smth. with smth.)*
    накры́ть (на) стол = *lay the table*
накры́ть *see* **накрыва́ть**
^в **нале́во** *to the left*
^с **налива́ть / нали́ть** (налью́, нальёт, налью́т; нале́й; на́лил, налила́, на́лило, на́лили)
    1) *pour out*

2) *fill*

нали́ть *see* налива́ть

нам *see* мы

^C наме́рение *intention*

на́ми *see* мы

^B наоборо́т
    1) *the other way round*
    2) *on the contrary*

напеча́тать *see* печа́тать

написа́ть *see* писа́ть

наплева́ть *see* плева́ть

^A напомина́ть / напо́мнить (напо́мню, напо́мнит, напо́мнят)
    1) (кому́ что *or* о чём) *remind (smb. of smth.)*
    2) (кому́ кого́) *remind (smb. of smb.)*

напо́мнить *see* напомина́ть

напра́виться *see* направля́ться

^B направле́ние
    1) *direction*
    2) *trend*

^B направля́ться / напра́виться (напра́влюсь, напра́вится, напра́вятся) *go*

^B напра́во *to the right*

^C напра́сно
    1) *in vain*
    2) *wrongfully, unjustly*

^A наприме́р *for example, for instance*

^B напро́тив
    1) *(adv.) opposite, on the contrary*
    2) *(prep. + gen.) opposite*

^C напряже́ние
    1) *straining*
    2) *tension*

^A напряжённый *strained, tense, strenuous*

нарисова́ть *see* рисова́ть

^A наро́д *people, nation*

^B наро́дный
    1) *people's*

2) *national*

3) *popular*

^B **наро́чно** *purposely, on purpose*

^C **наруша́ть** / **нару́шить** (нару́шу, нару́шит, нару́шат)

    1) *disturb, upset*

    2) *break, transgress*

    наруша́ть грани́цу = *illegally cross the frontier*

нару́шить *see* **наруша́ть**

^C **наря́дный** (наря́ден, наря́дна) *well-dressed, smart*

нас *see* **мы**

^C **населе́ние** *population*

^C **наско́лько**

    1) *how much*

    2) *as far as*

^C **насто́йчивый**

    1) *persistent*

    2) *urging*

^A **настоя́щий**

    1) *present*

    2) *real, genuine, true*

    по-настоя́щему = *really*

^B **настрое́ние** *mood, humour, frame of mind*

^A **наступа́ть** / **наступи́ть** (наступлю́, насту́пит, насту́пят)

    1) (на кого́ / что) *tread (upon smb. / smth.)*

    2) *(only ipf.) advance, be on the offensive*

    3) *(only in the 3rd pers.) set in, come (ab. time)*

наступи́ть *see* **наступа́ть**

^B **насчёт** *(prep. + gen.) as regards, concerning*

^A **нау́ка** *science, study*

научи́ть *see* **учи́ть**

научи́ться *see* **учи́ться**

нахму́риться *see* **хму́риться**

^A **находи́ть** (нахожу́, нахо́дит, нахо́дят) / **найти́** (найду́, найдёт, найду́т; нашёл, нашла́, нашло́, нашли́) *find*

^A **находи́ться** (нахожу́сь, нахо́дится, нахо́дятся) /

найти́сь (найду́сь, найдётся, найду́тся; нашёлся, нашла́сь, нашло́сь, нашли́сь)
1) *be found*
2) *(only pf.) find the right thing to do*

^C **национа́льный** *national*

^A **нача́ло** *beginning*

^A **нача́льник** *head, chief*

нача́ть *see* **начина́ть**

^A **начина́ть / нача́ть** (начну́, начнёт, начну́т; на́чал, начала́, на́чало, на́чали) *begin, start*

^A **наш** *(gen.* на́шего; *f.* на́ша, *gen.* на́шей; *n.* на́ше, *gen.* на́шего; *pl.* на́ши, *gen.* на́ших) *our, ours*

не́ *see* **не́чего**

^A **не** *not*

я не мог не сказа́ть = *I couldn't help saying*

небеса́ *see* **не́бо**

^A **не́бо** *(pl. nom.* небеса́, *gen.* небе́с, *dat.* небеса́м)
1) *sky*
2) *(mostly pl.) heaven*

^A **небольшо́й**
1) *not very big, not very large, not very great*
2) *small*

^C **неве́ста** *fiancee*

^B **нево́льный** *involuntary, unintentional*

^C **не́где** *there is nowhere*

^A **неда́вно** *recently, lately*

^B **недалёкий** (недалёк, недалека́, недалёко, недалёки) *not far off, (rather) near, (rather) short*

недалеко́ *see* **недалёкий**

^B **неда́ром**
1) *not without reason, not for nothing*
2) *not without purpose*

^A **неде́ля** *week*

^B **недоста́ток** *(gen.* недоста́тка)
1) *lack, shortage*
2) *shortcoming, defect*

^B **недоуме́ние** *bewilderment, perplexity*

^B **не́жный** (не́жен, нежна́, не́жно, не́жны́)

1) *tender, loving*

2) *delicate*

ней *see* **она́**

C **не́когда**

1) *there is no time*

2) *in former times*

A **не́который** *some, a certain*

A **нельзя́**

1) *it is impossible, one cannot*

2) *one must not*

мне нельзя́ чита́ть = *I must not read*

как нельзя́ лу́чше = *in the best way possible*

нём *see* **он** *and* **оно́**

B **нема́ло** *not a little, not a few, quite a number, a good deal, no little*

A **не́мец** *(gen.* не́мца*) German*

A **немно́го** *a little, some*

A **немно́жко** *a little, (just) a bit*

B **ненави́деть** (ненави́жу, ненави́дит, ненави́дят) *(ipf.) hate*

B **не́нависть** *(f.) hatred*

A **необходи́мый** *necessary, indispensable*

A **неожи́данный** *unexpected*

B **неподви́жный** (неподви́жен, неподви́жна) *immovable, motionless*

B **непреме́нно** *certainly, without fail*

B **не́рвный** (не́рвен, нервна́, не́рвно)

1) *(only the attributive forms) nerve, nervous*

2) *nervous*

A **не́сколько**

1) *some*

2) *somewhat*

B **несмотря́ на** *(prep. + acc.) in spite of*

A **нести́** (несу́, несёт, несу́т; нёс, несла́, несло́, несли́) *(det. vb. of motion) (ipf.)*

1) *carry*

2) *bear*

B **нести́сь** (несу́сь, несётся, несу́тся; нёсся, несла́сь, неслось, неслись) (ipf.) rush (along), scud (along)

^B **несча́стный** (несча́стен, несча́стна)

    1) *unhappy*

    2) *unfortunate*

    несча́стный слу́чай = *accident*

^A **нет**

    1) *no*

    2) *there is no, there are no, there is not, there are not*

    3) *(in reply to a negative question) yes*

    де́нег нет = *there is no money*

    у меня́ вре́мени нет = *I have no time*

^A **неуже́ли** *really, is it possible*

^C **неча́янный**

    1) *unintentional*

    2) *unexpected*

    неча́янный вы́стрел = *random shot*

^A **не́чего** *(dat.* не́чему, *instr.* не́чем, *the prepositional case* не́ о чем*) there is nothing*

    мне не́чего де́лать = *I have nothing to do*

    нам не́ о чем бы́ло говори́ть = *we had nothing to talk about*

  ни *see* **никто́** *and* **ничто́**

^A **ни**

    1) *(with a negation) not a (single)*

    2) *(without negation, preceded by* как, какой, что, куда, где*) (how)ever, (who)ever, (what)-ever, (where)ever*

    ни ..., ни = *neither ... nor*

    во что́ бы то ни ста́ло = *whatever the costs, at all costs*

    кто бы ни пришёл = *whoever comes*

^B **нигде́** *nowhere*

  ни́же *see* **ни́зкий**

^B **ни́жний** *lower*

^A **ни́зкий** (ни́зок, низка́, ни́зко, ни́зки; ни́же)

    1) *low*

    2) *base*

^A **ника́к** *in no way*
ника́к нельзя́ = *it is quite impossible*
^A **никако́й** *no ... (whatever), none ... (whatever)*
ни в како́м магази́не = *not in any shop*
^A **никогда́** *never*
^A **никто́** *(acc., gen.* никого́, *dat.* никому́, *instr.*
нике́м, *the prepositional case* ни о ком) *nobody,*
no one
об э́том я ни с кем не могу́ говори́ть = *I can*
speak to nobody about this
он ни о ком не хо́чет ду́мать = *he doesn't*
want to think about anybody
^B **никуда́** *nowhere*
^B **ниско́лько** *not at all, not in the least*
^A **ничего́**
1) *not bad*
2) *that is all right, never mind*
чу́вствовать себя́ ничего́ = *be (feeling) all*
right
ничего́ себе́ = *not so bad*
^A **ничто́** *(gen.* ничего́, *dat.* ничему́, *instr.* ниче́м,
the prepositional case ни о чём) *nothing*
он ни на что не спосо́бен = *he is no good*
он ни о чём не спра́шивает = *he does not ask*
about anything
^A **но** *but*
^A **но́вый** (нов, нова́, но́во, но́вы) *new, novel, modern*
^A **нога́** *(sg. acc.* но́гу, *gen.* ноги́, *pl. nom.* но́ги,
dat. нога́м)
1) *foot*
2) *leg*
^B **нож** *(E) knife*
^B **но́мер** *(pl.* номера́)
1) *number*
2) *hotel room*
^A **нос** (в, на, носу́; *pl. E) nose*
^A **носи́ть** (ношу́, но́сит, но́сят) *(indet. vb. of motion)*
(ipf.)

1) *carry*

2) *wear*

^C **носо́к** *(gen.* носка́*)*

1) *toe (of a shoe)*

2) *sock*

^B **ночева́ть** (ночу́ю, ночу́ет, ночу́ют), **пере-** *pass the night*

^A **ночь** *(f.)* (в ночи́; *gen. pl.* ноче́й) *night*

споко́йной но́чи! = *good night!*

но́чью = *at night*

^A **ноя́брь** *(gen.* ноября́*) November*

^A **нра́виться** (нра́влюсь, нра́вится, нра́вятся), **по-** (кому́ / чему́) *please (smb. / smth.)*

э́тот фильм мне нра́вится = *I like this film*

^A **ну** *now, come, well, suppose*

^C **нужда́** *(pl.* ну́жды*)*

1) *want, indigence*

2) *need*

^A **ну́жно** *it is necessary, one must, one should, one ought to*

нам ну́жно рабо́тать = *we have to work*

^A **ну́жный** (ну́жен, нужна́, ну́жно, нужны́) *necessary*

^B **ны́нешний** *present*

^B **ны́нче**

1) *today*

2) *now*

^C **ню́хать, по-** (что) *smell (at) (smth.)*

ню́хать таба́к = *take snuff*

^B **ня́ня** *nurse, nannie*

О

^A **о** (об, о́бо) *(prep. + acc. or the prepositional case)*

1) *(+ acc.) against, on, upon*

2) *(+ the prepositional case) about, of, on*

во́лны бью́тся о бе́рег = *the waves beat against the shore*

расска́зывать о стра́нном слу́чае = *tell about a strange case*

об *see* **о**

A **óба** *(gen. m. and n.* обóих; *f.* óбе, *gen.* обéих)
   both

B **обéд** *dinner*

A **обéдать, по-** *have dinner, dine*

   обернýть *see* **обёртывать**

B **обёртывать** *or* **оборáчивать / обернýть** (обернý,
   обернёт, обернýт)
      1) (что вокрýг чегó) *wind (smth. round smth.)*
      2) (что чем) *wrap (smth. up in smth.)*
      3) *turn*

A **обещáть** *(ipf. / pf. or pf.* **по-)** *promise*

B **обúда** *offence, injury, wrong*

   обúдеть *see* **обижáть**

B **обижáть / обúдеть** (обúжу, обúдит, обúдят)
      1) *offend*
      2) *harm*

B **óблако** *(pl. nom.* облакá *gen.* облакóв) *cloud*

B **óбласть** *(f.) (gen. pl.* областéй) *province, region,
   district*

B **облегчáть / облегчúть** (облегчý, облегчúт, облег-
   чáт)
      1) *lighten*
      2) *facilitate*
      3) *ease, relieve*
      4) *mitigate*

   облегчúть *see* **облегчáть**

   обманýть *see* **обмáнывать**

B **обмáнывать / обманýть** (обманý, обмáнет, об-
   мáнут) *deceive, cheat, trick*

B **обнарýживать / обнарýжить** (обнарýжу, обна-
   рýжит, обнарýжат)
      1) *display*
      2) *find, discover*
      3) *reveal*

   обнарýжить *see* **обнарýживать**

B **обнимáть / обнять** (обнимý, обнúмет, обнúмут;
   óбнял, обнялá, óбняло, óбняли) *embrace*

обня́ть *see* обнима́ть

о́бо *see* о

обойти́ *see* обходи́ть

обойти́сь *see* обходи́ться

обора́чивать *see* обёртывать

^C обору́дование *equipment*

обра́доваться *see* ра́доваться

^A о́браз

    1) *shape, form*

    2) *image*

    3) *manner*

    4) *(pl.* образа́*) icon*

    гла́вным о́бразом = *mainly*

образова́ть *see* образо́вывать

^B образо́вывать / образова́ть (образу́ю, образу́ет, образу́ют)

    1) *form, make up*

    2) *organize*

    3) *educate*

обрати́ть *see* обраща́ть

обрати́ться *see* обраща́ться

^B обра́тный

    1) *return*

    2) *reverse*

^B обраща́ть / обрати́ть (обращу́, обрати́т, обратя́т) *turn*

    обраща́ть внима́ние на что = *pay attention to something*

^A обраща́ться / обрати́ться (обращу́сь, обрати́тся, обратя́тся)

    1) (к кому́ / чему́) *apply (to smb. / smth.)*

    2) (во что) *turn (into smth.)*

обруга́ть *see* руга́ть

^B обстано́вка *(only sg.)*

    1) *furniture*

    2) *situation, atmosphere*

^B обстоя́тельство *circumstance*

обсуди́ть *see* обсужда́ть

^в **обсужда́ть / обсуди́ть** (обсужу́, обсу́дит, обсу́дят) *discuss*

обучи́ть *see* **учи́ть**

обучи́ться *see* **учи́ться**

^с **обходи́ть** (обхожу́, обхо́дит, обхо́дят) / **обойти́** (обойду́, обойдёт, обойду́т; обошёл, обошла́, обошло́, обошли́)
  1) *go round, walk round*
  2) *make the round, make one's round*
  3) *spread (all over) (for instance ab. news)*

^в **обходи́ться** (обхожу́сь, обхо́дится, обхо́дятся) / **обойти́сь** (обойду́сь, обойдётся, обойду́тся; обошёлся, обошла́сь, обошло́сь, обошли́сь)
  1) (с кем / чем) *treat (smb. / smth.)*
  2) (без кого́ / чего́) *manage (without smb. / smth.)*

^с **общежи́тие**
  1) *hostel*
  2) *(small) community*

^в **обще́ственный**
  1) *social*
  2) *public*

^в **о́бщество** *society*

^а **о́бщий**
  1) *general*
  2) *common*
  3) *aggregate, total*
  в о́бщем = *in general*

объяви́ть *see* **объявля́ть**

^в **объявля́ть / объяви́ть** (объявлю́, объя́вит, объя́вят) *declare, announce*

объясни́ть *see* **объясня́ть**

^а **объясня́ть / объясни́ть** (объясню́, объясни́т, объясня́т) *explain*

^а **обыкнове́нный** (обыкнове́нен, обыкнове́нна) *ordinary, usual*

^с **обы́чай** *custom*

^а **обы́чный** *usual, ordinary*

^B **обя́занный** *obliged*

^A **обяза́тельно** *by all means, certainly, without fail*

^C **овладева́ть / овладе́ть** (овладе́ю, овладе́ет, овладе́ют)
    1) (чем) *seize (smth.)*
    2) (чем) *master (smth.)*
  овладе́ть *see* **овладева́ть**

^B **огля́дываться / огляну́ться** (огляну́сь, огля́нет-ся, огля́нутся) *glance back*
  огляну́ться *see* **огля́дываться**

^A **огонёк** (огонька́)
    1) *small light, small fire*
    2) *enthusiasm*

^A **ого́нь** *(gen.* огня́*)*
    1) *fire*
    2) *light*

^C **огоро́д** *kitchen-garden*

^A **огро́мный** (огро́мен, огро́мна) *enormous, huge, vast*

^C **одева́ться / оде́ться** (оде́нусь, оде́нется, оде́нут-ся) *dress oneself*

^B **оде́жда** *(only sg.) clothes*

^A **оде́тый** *dressed*
  оде́ться *see* **одева́ться**

^B **одея́ло** *blanket*

^A **оди́н** *(gen.* одного́; *f.* одна́, *gen.* одно́й; *n.* одно́, *gen.* одного́; *pl.* одни́, *gen.* одни́х*)*
    1) *one*
    2) *one, the same, alone*
  в одно́й руба́шке = *(dressed) only in his shirt*
  все до одного́ = *all to a man*
  одни́ . . ., други́е = *some . . . some*

^C **одина́ковый** *identical, the same*

^B **оди́ннадцать** *(gen.* оди́ннадцати*) eleven*

^B **одино́кий**
    1) *lonely*
    2) *solitary*

^A **одна́жды** *once, one day*

^А одна́ко *however, but*

^С одновре́ме́нно *simultaneously*

одо́брить *see* одобря́ть

^С одобря́ть / одо́брить (одо́брю, одо́брит, одо́брят) *approve*

^В ожида́ть (кого́ / что *or* кого́ / чего́) *(ipf.) wait (for smb. / smth.), expect (smb. / smth.)*

^С озабо́ченный *preoccupied, anxious, worried*

^А о́зеро *(pl.* озёра*) lake*

оказа́ть *see* ока́зывать

оказа́ться *see* ока́зываться

^С ока́зывать / оказа́ть (окажу́, ока́жет, ока́жут) *render, show, exert, offer (assistance, resistance, etc.)*

^А ока́зываться / оказа́ться (окажу́сь, ока́жется, ока́жутся)
1) (кем / чем) *prove (to be) (smb. / smth.)*
2) *find oneself, be*

^А ока́нчивать / око́нчить (око́нчу, око́нчит, око́нчат) *finish, end*

^А окно́ *(pl. nom.* о́кна, *gen.* о́кон*) window*

^А о́коло *(prep. + gen.)*
1) *by, near, around*
2) *about*

око́нчить *see* ока́нчивать

окра́сить *see* кра́сить

^В окружа́ть / окружи́ть (окружу́, окружи́т, окружа́т) *surround*

окружи́ть *see* окружа́ть

^А октя́брь *(gen.* октября́*) October*

^А он *(acc., gen.* его́, *dat.* ему́, *instr.* им, *the prepositional case* о нём*) he; it (ab. masculines)*

^А она́ *(acc., gen.* её, *dat.* ей, *instr.* ей / е́ю, *the prepositional case* о ней*) she; it (ab. feminines)*

^А они́ *(acc., gen.* их, *dat.* им, *instr.* и́ми, *the prepositional case* о них*) they*

^А оно́ *(acc., gen.* его́, *dat.* ему́, *instr.* им, *the prepositional case* о нём*) it*

^C опа́здывать / опозда́ть *be late*

^B опа́сный (опа́сен, опа́сна) *dangerous*

^C о́пера *opera*

^C опера́ция *operation*

опере́ться *see* опира́ться

^B опира́ться / опере́ться (обопру́сь, обопрётся, обопру́тся; опёрся, опёрла́сь, опёрло́сь, опёрли́сь)

(на кого́ / что) *lean (upon smb. / smth.), rest (upon smb. / smth.)*

опозда́ть *see* опа́здывать

определи́ть *see* определя́ть

^B определя́ть / определи́ть (определю́, определи́т, определя́т)

1) *determine, define, estimate*

2) *appoint*

^B опуска́ть / опусти́ть (опущу́, опу́стит, опу́стят)

1) *lower, sink*

2) *drop*

опусти́ть *see* опуска́ть

^A о́пыт

1) *experience*

2) *experiment, test*

^A опя́ть *again*

^B организа́ция *organization*

^C организова́ть (организу́ю, организу́ет, организу́ют) *(ipf. / pf.) organize, arrange*

^C оре́х

1) *nut*

2) *nut-tree, walnut*

ему́ доста́лось на оре́хи = *he got it hot*

^B орке́стр *orchestra*

^B ору́жие *(only sg.) arm, weapon arms, weapons*

освети́ть *see* освеща́ть

^C освеща́ть / освети́ть (освещу́, освети́т, осветя́т)

1) (кого́ / что) *light (smb. / smth.)*

2) (что) *throw light (upon smth.)*

освободи́ть *see* освобожда́ть

^в **освобожда́ть / освободи́ть** (освобожу́, освободи́т, освободя́т)
 1) *liberate, set free*
 2) *free, relieve, release*
 3) *vacate*
^в **осе́нний** *autumn, autumnal*
^а **о́сень** *(f.) autumn*
 о́сенью = *in autumn*
 оскорби́ть *see* **оскорбля́ть**
^в **оскорбля́ть / оскорби́ть** (оскорблю́, оскорби́т, оскорбя́т) *insult*
 ослабе́ть *see* **слабе́ть**
^в **осма́тривать / осмотре́ть** (осмотрю́, осмо́трит, осмо́трят)
 1) *see, inspect*
 2) *examine*
 осмотре́ть *see* **осма́тривать**
^с **основа́ние**
 1) *foundation*
 2) *base, bed(ding), root, foot*
 3) *grounds, reason*
 4) *base (chemistry, mathematics)*
^в **основно́й** *fundamental, basic*
^а **осо́бенный** *special, especial, particular*
^в **осо́бый**
 1) *special, particular*
 2) *peculiar*
^а **остава́ться** (остаю́сь, остаётся, остаю́тся) / **оста́ться** (оста́нусь, оста́нется, оста́нутся)
 1) *remain, stay*
 2) *be left*
 оста́вить *see* **оставля́ть**
^а **оставля́ть / оста́вить** (оста́влю, оста́вит, оста́вят) *leave*
 оста́вить за собо́й пра́во = *reserve (for) (oneself) the right*
 оста́вь(те)! = *stop that!*
^а **остально́й** *the rest (of)*

^A **остана́вливать / останови́ть** (остановлю́, оста-
    но́вит, остано́вят) *stop*
  останови́ть *see* **остана́вливать**
^C **остано́вка** *(gen. pl.* остано́вок*)*
    1) *stop, halt*
    2) *stop, station*
  оста́ться *see* **остава́ться**
^A **осторо́жный** (осторо́жен, осторо́жна) *careful,
    cautious*
^B **о́стров** *(pl.* острова́*) island*
^A **о́стрый**
    1) (остр, остра́, о́стро) *sharp*
    2) (остёр, остра́) *keen, sharp*
    3) *(only attributive forms) acute, stinging*
    о́строе положе́ние = *critical situation*
  осуществи́ть *see* **осуществля́ть**
^C **осуществля́ть / осуществи́ть** (осуществлю́, о-
    существи́т, осуществя́т) *carry out, realize*
^A **от** (о́то) *(prep.* + *gen.)*
    1) *from*
    2) *for, with*
    3) *against*
    4) *to*
    он уе́хал от дете́й = *he went away from the
    children*
    петь от ра́дости = *sing for joy*
    защи́та от врага́ = *defence against the enemy*
    ключ от ко́мнаты = *a key to the room*
  отверну́ться *see* **отвёртываться**
^C **отвёртываться** *or* **отвора́чиваться / отверну́ться**
    (отверну́сь, отвернётся, отверну́тся) *turn
    away*
^A **отве́т** *answer, reply*
  отве́тить *see* **отвеча́ть**
^B **отве́тственный** *responsible*
^A **отвеча́ть / отве́тить** (отве́чу, отве́тит, отве́тят)
    answer, reply
    отве́тить уро́к = *say one's lesson, be examined*

отвора́чиваться *see* **отвёртываться**

^В **отдава́ть** (отдаю́, отдаёт, отдаю́т; отдава́й) / **отда́ть** (отда́м, отда́шь, отда́ст, отдади́м, отдади́те, отдаду́т; отда́й; о́тдал, отдала́, о́тдало, о́тдали)
   1) *return, give back*
   2) *give, give up*

отда́ть *see* **отдава́ть**

^В **отделе́ние**
   1) *department, branch, section*
   2) *separation*

^А **отде́льный** *separate*

отдохну́ть *see* **отдыха́ть**

^В **о́тдых** *rest, relaxation*

^А **отдыха́ть** / **отдохну́ть** (отдохну́, отдохнёт, отдохну́т)
   1) *rest*
   2) *have a holiday*

^А **оте́ц** *(gen.* отца́*) father*

^С **оте́чественный** *native, home*

отказа́ться *see* **отка́зываться**

^А **отка́зываться** / **отказа́ться** (откажу́сь, отка́жется, отка́жутся)
   (от чего́) *refuse (smth.), renounce (smth.)*
   отказа́ться от свои́х слов = *go back on one's words*

^В **открове́нный** (открове́нен открове́нна)
   1) *sincere*
   2) *frank*

^А **открыва́ть** / **откры́ть** (откро́ю, откро́ет, откро́ют)
   1) *open*
   2) *discover*

^А **откры́тый**
   1) *open*
   2) *frank*

откры́ть *see* **открыва́ть**

^А **отку́да** *where … from*

^C **отку́да-то** *from somewhere*

^B **отлича́ться / отличи́ться** (отличу́сь, отличи́тся, отлича́тся)
1) *distinguish oneself*
2) *be notable*
3) *differ*

отличи́ться *see* **отлича́ться**

^A **отли́чный** (отли́чен, отли́чна) *excellent*
отли́чно = "*full marks*"

отме́тить *see* **отмеча́ть**

^B **отмеча́ть / отме́тить** (отме́чу, отме́тит, отме́тят)
1) *mark off*
2) *mark*
3) *note*

отнести́сь *see* **относи́ться**

^C **отнима́ть / отня́ть** (отниму́, отни́мет, отни́мут; о́тнял, отняла́, о́тняло, о́тняли)
1) (кого́ / что у кого́ / чего́) *take (smb. | smth.) away (from smb. | smth.)*
2) (что от чего́) *subtract (smth. from smth.)*

^C **относи́тельно** *(prep. + gen.) concerning*

^A **относи́ться** (отношу́сь, отно́сится, отно́сятся) / **отнести́сь** (отнесу́сь, отнесётся, отнесу́тся; отнёсся, отнесла́сь, отнесло́сь, отнесли́сь) (к кому́ / чему́) 1) *treat (smb. | smth.)* 2) *think of (smb. | smth)* 3) *have to do (with smb. | smth.)* 4) *(only ipf.) date (from smth.)*

^A **отноше́ние**
1) *attitude*
2) *relation*
3) *relations*

отня́ть *see* **отнима́ть**

о́то *see* **от**

отойти́ *see* **отходи́ть**

отпра́вить *see* **отправля́ть**

отпра́виться *see* **отправля́ться**

^C **отправля́ть / отпра́вить** (отпра́влю, отпра́вит, отпра́вят) *send, forward*

^B **отправля́ться / отпра́виться** (отпра́влюсь, от-

пра́вится, отпра́вятся) *set off, start*

^C **о́тпуск** (в о́тпуске / в отпуску́; *pl.* отпуска́) *leave (of absence), holiday*

^B **отпуска́ть** / **отпусти́ть** (отпущу́, отпу́стит, отпу́стят)
    1) *let go, set free, release*
    2) *slacken*

    отпусти́ть *see* **отпуска́ть**

^C **отража́ть** / **отрази́ть** (отражу́, отрази́т, отразя́т)
    1) *repulse, repel*
    2) *reflect*

    отрази́ть *see* **отража́ть**

    отруга́ть *see* **руга́ть**

^B **отря́д** *detachment, vanguard*

^B **отстава́ть** (отстаю́, отстаёт, отстаю́т; отстава́й) / **отста́ть** (отста́ну, отста́нет, отста́нут)
    1) (от кого́ / чего́) *be, fall (behind smb. / smth.)*
    2) (от чего́) *miss (smth.)*
    3) *(only in the 3rd pers.) be slow (ab. clock)*

    отста́ть *see* **отстава́ть**

^C **отсу́тствовать** (отсу́тствую, отсу́тствует, отсу́тствуют) *(ipf.) be absent*

^A **отсю́да** *from here, hence*

^A **отту́да** *from there*

^A **отходи́ть** (отхожу́, отхо́дит, отхо́дят) / **отойти́** (отойду́, отойдёт, отойду́т; отошёл, отошла́, отошло́, отошли́)
    1) (от кого́ / чего́) *go, move (away from smb. / smth.)*
    2) *leave*

^B **отча́яние** *despair*

^B **отчего́** *why*

^C **о́тчество** *patronymic*

^C **отъе́зд** *departure*

^B **офице́р** *officer*

    охвати́ть *see* **охва́тывать**

^C **охва́тывать** / **охвати́ть** (охвачу́, охва́тит, охва́тят)

1) *seize, grip*
2) *envelop*
3) *comprehend*
4) *include*

^C **охо́та**
   1) *hunt, hunting, chase*
   2) *wish, inclination*
   охо́та тебе́! = *it beats me why you go to the trouble of doing it!*
   с охо́той = *with pleasure*

^B **охо́титься** (охо́чусь, охо́тится, охо́тятся) *(ipf.)*
   (на кого́ / что *or* за кем / чем)
   1) *hunt (smb. / smth.)*
   2) *hunt (for smb. / smth.)*

^B **очеви́дно** *obviously, apparently*

^A **о́чень** *very, very much, greatly*

^B **очередно́й**
   1) *next (in turn)*
   2) *usual, regular, recurrent*

^B **о́чередь** *(f.)* *(gen. pl.* очереде́й)
   1) *(one's) turn*
   2) *queue*

очи́стить *see* **чи́стить**

^B **очки́** *(only pl.; gen.* очко́в) *(pair of) spectacles*

^B **ошиба́ться / ошиби́ться** (ошибу́сь, ошибётся, ошибу́тся; оши́бся, оши́блась, оши́блось, оши́блись) *make a mistake, be mistaken*

ошиби́ться *see* **ошиба́ться**

^A **оши́бка** *(gen. pl.* оши́бок) *mistake, error*

ощути́ть *see* **ощуща́ть**

^B **ощуща́ть / ощути́ть** (ощущу́, ощути́т, ощутя́т) *feel, sense*

П

^A **па́дать / упа́сть** *or* **пасть** ((у)паду́, (у)падёт, (у)паду́т; (у)па́л, (у)па́ла, (у)па́ло, (у)па́ли) *fall*

па́дать ду́хом = *lose courage*

C **паке́т** *package, parcel, packet*

C **пала́та**
1) *(old) palace*
2) *ward*
3) *chamber (in legislative assembly)*
4) *chamber (of commerce, etc.)*

A **па́лец** *(gen.* па́льца) *finger, toe*

C **па́лка** *(gen. pl.* па́лок) *stick*

A **пальто́** *(indeclinable n.) (over)coat*

C **па́мятник** *monument, memorial*

A **па́мять** *(f.)*
1) *memory*
2) *recollection, remembrance*

A **па́па** *dad*

B **папиро́са** *cigarette*

B **па́ра** *pair, couple*

A **па́рень** *(gen. sg.* па́рня, *gen. pl.* парне́й) *fellow, lad, chap*

C **парикма́хер** *hairdresser, barber*

A **парк**
1) *park*
2) *fleet, stock*

B **парохо́д** *steamer*

C **па́рта** *desk (at school)*

C **партиза́н** *(gen. pl.* партиза́н) *partisan*

B **па́ртия**
1) *party*
2) *detachment*
3) *batch, lot*
4) *(good) match*

C **па́смурный** (па́смурен, па́смурна)
1) *cloudy, dull, overcast*
2) *gloomy*

B **пассажи́р** *passenger*

пасть *see* па́дать

B **па́уза** *pause, interval*

B **па́хнуть** (па́хну, па́хнет, па́хнут; па́х(нул)

пáх(ну)ла, пáх(ну)ло, пáх(ну)ли) *(ipf.)*
(чем) *smell (of smth.)*

^C **певе́ц** *(gen.* певца́*) singer*

^C **певи́ца** *singer (ab. woman)*

^A **пе́рвый** *first, former*
во-пе́рвых = *in the first place, first of all, for one thing, firstly*

^B **перебива́ть / переби́ть** (перебью́, перебьёт, пе-ребью́т; перебе́й) *interrupt*

переби́ть *see* **перебива́ть**

перевести́ *see* **переводи́ть**

^C **переводи́ть** (перевожу́, перево́дит, перево́дят) / **перевести́** (переведу́, переведёт, переведу́т; перевёл, перевела́, перевело́, перевели́)
1) (кого́ / что че́рез что) *take, lead (smb. / smth.) across (smth.)*
2) *transfer*
3) *translate*

^A **пе́ред** (пе́редо) *(prep.* + *instr.)*
1) *before*
2) *in front of*

^A **передава́ть** (передаю́, передаёт, передаю́т) / **переда́ть** (переда́м, переда́шь, переда́ст, пе-редади́м, передади́те, передаду́т; переда́й; пе́редал, передала́, пе́редало, пе́редали)
1) *pass, give*
2) *broadcast*
3) *tell*

переда́ть *see* **передава́ть**

^B **переда́ча** *transmission*

^B **пере́дний** *front, first, foreground*
пере́дняя = *anteroom, antechamber*

пе́редо *see* **пе́ред**

^C **передово́й**
1) *foremost, forward, advanced*
2) *progressive*
3) *progressive-minded*
передова́я (статья́) = *leading article*

ᶜ **переезжа́ть / перее́хать** (перее́ду, перее́дет, пере́едут)
  1) (что *or* че́рез что) *drive across, cross (smth.)*
  2) *move*
перее́хать *see* **переезжа́ть**
ᶜ **пережива́ть / пережи́ть** (переживу́, переживёт,
переживу́т; пе́режи́л, пережила́, пе́режи́ло, пе́
режи́ли)
  1) *experience*
  2) (кого́) *outlive (smb.)*
  3) *get through, recover from*
  4) *endure*
пережи́ть *see* **пережива́ть**
перейти́ *see* **переходи́ть**
ᴮ **переме́на**
  1) *change*
  2) *interval, break, recess*
перенести́ *see* **переноси́ть**
ᴮ **переноси́ть** (переношу́, перено́сит, перено́сят) /
перенести́ (перенесу́, перенесёт, перенесу́т;
перенёс, перенесла́, перенесло́, перенесли́)
  1) (кого́ / что че́рез что) *carry (smb. / smth.)*
  across (smth.)
  2) *carry somewhere else*
  3) *transfer*
  4) *put off, postpone*
  5) *endure*
переночева́ть *see* **ночева́ть**
ᶜ **переры́в** *interruption, break*
ᴬ **перестава́ть** (перестаю́, перестаёт, перестаю́т) /
переста́ть (переста́ну, переста́нет, переста́нут)
stop, cease
переста́ть *see* **перестава́ть**
ᴮ **переу́лок** *(gen.* переу́лка*) by-street, lane, alley*
ᴬ **переходи́ть** (перехожу́, перехо́дит, перехо́дят) /
перейти́ (перейду́, перейдёт, перейду́т; перешёл, перешла́, перешло́, перешли́)
  1) (что *or* че́рез что) *cross (smth.)*

2) *change*

3) (во что, к чему *or* на что) *pass on (to smth.)*

^C **пери́од** *period*

^C **перо́** *(pl. nom.* пе́рья, *gen.* пе́рьев)
1) *feather*
2) *pen*

^C **перча́тка** *(gen. pl.* перча́ток) *glove*

^A **пе́сня** *(gen. pl.* пе́сен) *song*

^B **песо́к** *(gen.* песка́) *sand*

^A **петь** (пою́, поёт, пою́т), **про-, с-** *sing*

^B **печа́льный** (печа́лен, печа́льна)
1) *sad, mournful*
2) *grievous*

^C **печа́тать, на-** *print*

^A **пече́нье** *pastry, biscuits*

^C **пе́чка** *(gen. pl.* пе́чек) *stove, oven, heater, furnace*

^B **печь** (в печи́; *gen. pl.* пече́й)
1) *stove*
2) *furnace*

^B **пешко́м** *on foot*

^C **пиджа́к** *(E) coat, jacket*

^A **пионе́р**
1) *pioneer*
2) *Young Pioneer (member of the Soviet Russian Children's Pioneer Association)*

^C **пиро́г** *(E) pie, tart*

^B **пиро́жное** *(adj. used substantively) pastry, fancy cake*

^B **писа́тель** *(m.) writer, author*

^A **писа́ть** (пишу́, пи́шет, пи́шут), **на-**
1) *write*
2) *paint*

^A **письмо́** *(pl. nom.* пи́сьма, *gen.* пи́сем) *letter*

^A **пить** (пью, пьёт, пьют; пей; пил, пила́, пи́ло, пи́ли), **вы-** *drink, take*

^B **пла́вать** *(indet. vb. of motion) (ipf.) swim, sail*

^A **пла́кать** (пла́чу, пла́чет, пла́чут) *(ipf.) weep, cry*

^C **пла́мя** *(gen., dat., the prepositional case* пла́мени,

instr. пла́менем) *flame*

^A **план** *plan*

^C **плати́ть** (плачу́, пла́тит, пла́тят), **за-, у-**
    1) *(pf.* за-, у-) (за кого́ / что) *pay (for smb. / smth.)*
    2) *(pf.* за-) (чем за что) *return (smth. for smth.)*

^A **плато́к** *(gen.* платка́) *shawl, kerchief*

^C **платфо́рма**
    1) *platform*
    2) *halt*
    3) *truck*
    4) *platform (politics)*

^A **пла́тье** *(gen. pl.* пла́тьев)
    1) *dress, gown, frock*
    2) *(only sg.) clothes*

^C **плева́ть** (плюю́, плюёт, плюю́т) **на-,** *or* **плю́нуть**
    (плю́ну, плю́нет, плю́нут)
    1) *spit*
    2) *not care a straw*
    плева́ть в потоло́к = *sit twiddling one's thumbs*

^A **плечо́** *(pl. nom.* пле́чи, *gen.* плеч, *dat.* плеча́м)
    shoulder
    э́то ему́ не по плечу́ = *that is beyond his power*

^C **пло́тный** (пло́тен, плотна́, пло́тно)
    1) *compact, dense*
    2) *thickset*
    3) *solid, strong*

^A **плохо́й** (плох, плоха́, пло́хо; ху́же) *bad*

^B **площа́дка** *(gen. pl.* площа́док)
    1) *ground*
    2) *platform*

^A **пло́щадь** *(f.) (gen. pl.* площаде́й)
    1) *square*
    2) *area*

^C **плыть** (плыву́, плывёт, плыву́т; плыл, плыла́,
    плы́ло, плы́ли) *(det. vb. of motion) swim, sail*

плю́нуть *see* **плева́ть**

^C **пляж** *beach*

по *(prep. + dat., acc. or the prepositional case)*
  (+ dat.)
  1) *on, along, in, all over, about*
  2) *by, according to*
  3) *(with reference to means of communication or
      conveyance) by, over*
  4) *(with reference to activities) in*
  5) *(ab. recurring time) in, on*
  6) *(indicating distribution) each, apiece*
  7) *(ab. purpose) on*
  (+ acc.) to, up to
  (+ the prepositional case) on
  ходи́ть по доро́ге = *walk along the road*
  ходи́ть по у́лицам = *walk about the streets*
  рабо́тать по пла́ну = *work according to the
      plan*
  по по́чте = *by post*
  специали́ст по исто́рии = *expert in history*
  по вечера́м = *in the evening*
  дать всем по я́блоку = *give them an apple each*
  он уе́хал по дела́м = *he went away on business*
  с второ́го по девя́тое число́ = *from the 1st to
      the 9th*
  по получе́нии письма́ = *on receiving the letter*
A **побе́да** *victory*
C **победи́тель** *(m.) conqueror, victor*
  победи́ть *see* **побежда́ть**
B **побежда́ть** / **победи́ть** *(no 1st pers. sg.,* победи́т,
    победя́т*) conquer, win a victory*
  поби́ть *see* **бить**
  поблагодари́ть *see* **благодари́ть**
  побледне́ть *see* **бледне́ть**
  побри́ть *see* **брить**
B **побыва́ть** *(pf.)*
  1) *travel about*
  2) *be, stay, live (for some time)*
C **поведе́ние** *conduct, behaviour*
C **повезти́** (повезу́, повезёт, повезу́т; повёз, по-

везла́, повезло́, повезли́) *(pf.)* *(begin to)* *convey, (begin to) carry*

тебе́ повезло́ = *you have been lucky*

поверну́ть *see* **повёртывать**

В **повёртывать** *or* **повора́чивать / поверну́ть** (поверну́, повернёт, поверну́т) *turn, swing*

пове́сить *see* **ве́шать**

С **по́весть** *(f.)* *short story, narrative*

повида́ть *see* **вида́ть**

В **по-ви́димому** *apparently, to all appearance*

С **по́вод** *occasion, cause, ground*

повора́чивать *see* **повёртывать**

С **поворо́т**
1) *turn(ing), bend, curve*
2) *turning-point*

повтори́ть *see* **повторя́ть**

А **повторя́ть / повтори́ть** (повторю́, повтори́т, повторя́т) *repeat*

погаси́ть *see* **гаси́ть**

А **погиба́ть / поги́бнуть** (поги́бну, поги́бнет, поги́бнут; поги́б(нул), поги́б(ну)ла, поги́б(ну)ло, поги́б(ну)ли) *perish, be killed*

поги́бнуть *see* **ги́бнуть** *and* **погиба́ть**

погла́дить *see* **гла́дить**

погляде́ть *see* **гляде́ть**

С **погля́дывать** *(ipf.)*
(на кого́ / что) *look (at smb. / smth.)*

А **пого́да** *weather*

погрози́ть *see* **грози́ть**

погуля́ть *see* **гуля́ть**

А **под** (по́до) *(prep. + acc. or instr.)*
(+ acc.)
1) *under*
2) *(ab. time) towards, on the eve of, close upon*
3) *to (the accompaniment of)*
(+ instr.)
1) *under*
2) *in the environs of*

поста́вить под стол = *put under the table*
под ве́чер = *towards evening*
ему́ под со́рок = *he is close upon forty*
танцева́ть под му́зыку = *dance to the music*
лежа́ть под столо́м = *lie under the table*
под Москво́й = *in the environs of Moscow*

ᴬ **подава́ть** (подаю́, подаёт, подаю́т; подава́й) /
пода́ть (пода́м, пода́шь, пода́ст, подади́м,
подади́те, подаду́т; пода́й; по́дал, подала́,
по́дало, по́дали)

1) (что кому́) *help (smb. on with smth.)*
2) *serve*
3) *hold out, offer*
4) *drive up (to the door), come in (ab. train)*

подари́ть *see* **дари́ть**

ᴬ **пода́рок** *(gen.* пода́рка*) present, gift*

пода́ть *see* **подава́ть**

ᶜ **подбега́ть** / **подбежа́ть** (подбегу́, подбежи́т, под-
бегу́т) (к кому́ / чему́) *run up (to smb. | smth.)*

подбежа́ть *see* **подбега́ть**

ᴮ **подборо́док** *(gen.* подборо́дка*) chin*

ᴮ **по́двиг** *exploit, feat*

ᶜ **подгото́вка** *preparation*

поддержа́ть *see* **подде́рживать**

ᴮ **подде́рживать** / **поддержа́ть** (поддержу́, подде́р-
жит, подде́ржат)

1) *support, back up*
2) *maintain*

поде́йствовать *see* **де́йствовать**

подели́ть *see* **дели́ть**

поднести́ *see* **подноси́ть**

ᴬ **поднима́ть** / **подня́ть** (подниму́, подни́мет, под-
ни́мут; по́днял, подняла́, по́дняло, по́дняли) *lift,
raise, pick up*

ᴬ **поднима́ться** / **подня́ться** (поднplusму́сь, подни́мет-
ся, подни́мутся; подня́лся, подняла́сь, подня-
ло́сь, подняли́сь)

1) (на что) *climb (smth.), ascend (smth.),*

(по чему́) *go up (smth.)*

2) *rise, get up*

3) *go up*

^C **подноси́ть** (подношу́, подно́сит, подно́сят) / **поднести́** (поднесу́, поднесёт, поднесу́т; поднёс, поднесла́, поднесло́, поднесли́)

    1) (кого́ / что к кому́ / чему́) *carry, bring (smb. | smth. to smb. | smth.)*

    2) (кому́ / чему́ что) *present (smb. | smth. with smth.)*

подня́ть *see* **поднима́ть**

подня́ться *see* **поднима́ться**

по́до *see* **под**

^A **подо́бный** (подо́бен, подо́бна) *like, similar, such a*

    и тому́ подо́бное *(abbreviated:* и т.п.*)* = *and so on*

^B **подожда́ть** (подожду́, подождёт, подожду́т; подожда́л, подождала́, подожда́ло, подожда́ли) *(pf.)*

    (кого́ / что *or* кого́ / чего́) *wait (for smb. | smth.)*

подойти́ *see* **подходи́ть**

^C **подро́бный** (подро́бен, подро́бна) *detailed*

^A **подру́га** *(female) friend*

подтверди́ть *see* **подтвержда́ть**

^C **подтвержда́ть** / **подтверди́ть** (подтвержу́, подтверди́т, подтвердя́т) *confirm, corroborate*

поду́мать *see* **ду́мать**

^B **поду́шка** *(gen. pl.* поду́шек*) pillow, cushion*

подхвати́ть *see* **подхва́тывать**

^B **подхва́тывать** / **подхвати́ть** (подхвачу́, подхва́тит, подхва́тят)

    1) *pick up*

    2) *catch*

    3) *catch up, join in*

^A **подходи́ть** (подхожу́, подхо́дит, подхо́дят) / **подойти́** (подойду́, подойдёт, подойду́т; подошёл, подошла́, подошло́, подошли́)

1) (к комý / чемý) *go up (to smb. / smth.),*
come up (to smb. / smth.)

2) (комý) *do (for smb.), fit (smb.), suit (smb.)*

^C подъéзд

1) *drive*

2) *porch, entrance, doorway*

^C подъезжáть / подъéхать (подъéду, подъéдет,
подъéдут)

(к комý / чемý) *drive up (to smb. / smth.)*

^C подъём

1) *lifting*

2) *ascent*

3) *slope, upgrade*

4) *raising, development*

5) *enthusiasm*

подъéхать *see* подъезжáть

^A пóезд *(pl.* поездá*) train*

^B поéздка *(gen. pl.* поéздок*) journey*

^A поéхать (поéду, поéдет, поéдут; поезжáй) *(pf.)*
(begin to) drive, (begin to) ride, set off, depart
поéхали! = *let's be going!*

пожалéть *see* жалéть

пожáловаться *see* жáловаться

^B пожáлуй *perhaps, very likely, may, I think that*
пожáлуй, он придёт = *I think he will come*

^A пожáлуйста

1) *please*

2) *don't mention it, not at all*

3) *certainly; not translated*

^C пожáр *fire*

пожáть *see* пожимáть

пожелáть *see* желáть

^C пожилóй *elderly*

^B пожимáть / пожáть (пожмý, пожмёт, пожмýт)
press (a little)
пожáть плечáми = *shrug one's shoulders*

позабóтиться *see* забóтиться

позавúдовать *see* завúдовать

поза́втракать *see* **за́втракать**

^C **позавчера́** *the day before yesterday*

позва́ть *see* **звать**

позво́лить *see* **позволя́ть**

^B **позволя́ть** / **позво́лить** (позво́лю, позво́лит, позво́лят)

(кому́ / чему́ что) *allow, permit (smb. | smth. (to do) smth.)*

позво́ль, что тако́е ты говори́шь? = *permit me to ask what you are talking about*

позвони́ть *see* **звони́ть**

^A **по́здний** (поздне́е *or* по́зже) *late*

поздоро́ваться *see* **здоро́ваться**

поздра́вить *see* **поздравля́ть**

^C **поздравля́ть** / **поздра́вить** (поздра́влю, поздра́вит, поздра́вят)

(кого́ / что с чем) *congratulate (smb. | smth. on smth.)*

по́зже *see* **по́здний**

познако́миться *see* **знако́миться**

^B **по́иск**

1) *search*

2) *(only pl.) reconnaissance, scouting*

пойма́ть *see* **лови́ть**

^A **пойти́** (пойду́, пойдёт, пойду́т; пошёл, пошла́, пошло́, пошли́) *(pf.) (begin to) go, (begin to) walk*

пошёл! = *off with you! begone!*

пошли́! = *come on! let us go now!*

^A **пока́**

1) *for the present, for the time being*

2) *yet*

3) *while*

4) *(in sentences containing a negation) until, till*

пока́! = *so long!*

показа́ть *see* **пока́зывать**

^A **пока́зывать** / **показа́ть** (покажу́, пока́жет, пока́жут)

1) *show*

2) (на кого / что) *point (at smb. / smth.)*

поклони́ться *see* **кла́няться**

^в **поко́й** *rest, peace*

мы оста́вим его́ в поко́е = *we will leave him alone*

поколеба́ться *see* **колеба́ться**

^с **поколе́ние** *generation*

покорми́ть *see* **корми́ть**

покра́сить *see* **кра́сить**

покрасне́ть *see* **красне́ть**

^в **покрыва́ть / покры́ть** (покро́ю, покро́ет, покро́ют)

1) *cover*

2) *defray*

3) *conceal*

орке́стр покры́л шум = *the orchestra drowned the noise*

покры́ть *see* **покрыва́ть**

^А **покупа́ть / купи́ть** (куплю́, ку́пит, ку́пят) *buy*

поку́шать *see* **ку́шать**

^А **пол** (на полу́; *pl. E*) *floor*

пол- *see* **пол(у)-**

^в **полага́ть** (*ipf.*) *suppose*

^А **по́ле** (*pl. nom.* поля́, *gen.* поле́й)

1) *field*

2) *ground*

3) (*mostly pl.*) *margin*

4) (*mostly pl.*) *brim*

^А **поле́зный** (поле́зен, поле́зна) *useful*

^в **полити́ческий** *political*

^с **поли́ция** *police*

^с **по́лка** (*gen. pl.* по́лок)

1) *shelf*

2) *berth (in sleeping-car)*

^с **полко́вник** *colonel*

^А **по́лный** (по́лон, полна́, по́лно, по́лны́)

1) *full, packed*

2) *complete, total*

3) *absolute, perfect*

4) *stout, corpulent*

^A полови́на *half*

в полови́не второ́го = *at half past one*

^A положе́ние

    1) *position*

    2) *posture, attitude*

    3) *condition, situation*

положи́ть *see* класть

полома́ть *see* лома́ть

^B полоса́ *(sg. acc.* по́лосу, *gen.* полосы́, *pl. nom.* по́лосы, *gen.* поло́с, *dat.* полоса́м) *stripe*

^B полтора́ *(f.* полторы́; *gen. m., f., n.* полу́тора) *one and a half*

^B пол(у)- *half-, semi-*

^A получа́ть / получи́ть (получу́, полу́чит, полу́чат) *receive, get, obtain*

^A получа́ться / получи́ться *(only in the 3rd pers.:* полу́чится, полу́чатся)

    1) *come*

    2) *turn out, be*

получи́ть *see* получа́ть

получи́ться *see* получа́ться

^B полчаса́ *(m.) (gen.* получа́са) *half an hour*

^B по́льза *use*

^B по́льзоваться (по́льзуюсь, по́льзуется, по́льзуются), вос-

(чем)

    1) *(only ipf.) use (smth.)*

    2) *profit (by smth.)*

    3) *(only ipf.) enjoy (smth.)*

полюбова́ться *see* любова́ться

поменя́ться *see* меня́ться

помести́ть *see* помеща́ть

помеша́ть *see* меша́ть

^B помеща́ть / помести́ть (помещу́, помести́т, помести́т)

1) *place*
2) *invest*
3) *insert*
4) *accomodate*

ᴮ **помеще́ние** *room, premises*

ᶜ **поме́щик** *landed gentleman, lord of the manor*

ᴬ **по́мнить** (по́мню, по́мнит, по́мнят) *(ipf.)* (кого́ / что *or* о ком / чём) *remember (smb. / smth.)*

ᴬ **помога́ть / помо́чь** (помогу́, помо́жет, помо́гут; помо́г, помогла́, помогло́, помогли́) (кому́ / чему́) *help (smb. / smth.)*

по-мо́ему *see* **мой**

помо́чь *see* **помога́ть**

ᴮ **помо́щник** *assistant*

ᴬ **по́мощь** *(f.) help, assistance*

помы́ть *see* **мыть**

ᴬ **понеде́льник** *Monday*

ᶜ **понести́** (понесу́, понесёт, понесу́т; понёс, понесла́, понесло́, понесли́)
1) *(begin to) carry*
2) *bolt (ab. horse)*

ᴬ **понима́ть / поня́ть** (пойму́, поймёт, пойму́т; по́нял, поняла́, по́няло, по́няли) *understand*

понра́виться *see* **нра́виться**

поню́хать *see* **ню́хать**

ᶜ **поня́тие** *idea, notion*

ᴬ **поня́тный** (поня́тен, поня́тна) *intelligible, clear, sensible*

поня́ть *see* **понима́ть**

пообе́дать *see* **обе́дать**

пообеща́ть *see* **обеща́ть**

ᶜ **поп** *(gen.* попа́*) (Russian) priest*

ᴬ **попада́ть / попа́сть** (попаду́, попадёт, попаду́т; попа́л, попа́ла, попа́ло, попа́ли)
1) (в кого́ / во что) *hit (smb. / smth.)*
2) *get, find oneself*
как попа́ло = *anyhow*
ему́ попа́ло = *he got it hot*

попа́сть *see* **попада́ть**

попра́вить *see* **поправля́ть**

B **поправля́ть / попра́вить** (попра́влю, попра́вит, попра́вят)
   1) *correct*
   2) *set straight, readjust*
   3) *repair, mend*
   4) *improve*

B **по-пре́жнему** *as before, as usual*

попро́бовать *see* **про́бовать**

попроси́ть *see* **проси́ть**

A **пора́** *(acc.* по́ру, *gen.* поры́, *pl.* по́ры*) time*
   пора́ = *it is time*

B **поража́ть / порази́ть** (поражу́, порази́т, порази́т)
   1) *beat, conquer*
   2) *hit*
   3) *strike, startle*

порази́ть *see* **поража́ть**

B **поро́г** *threshold*

C **порт** (в порту́; *gen. pl.* порто́в) *port*

B **портре́т** *portrait*

C **портфе́ль** *(m.)*
   1) *briefcase*
   2) *portfolio*

A **поря́док** *(gen.* поря́дка*) order, sequence*

посади́ть *see* **сажа́ть**

посвети́ть *see* **свети́ть**

посвяти́ть *see* **посвяща́ть**

C **посвяща́ть / посвяти́ть** (посвящу́, посвяти́т, посвятя́т)
   1) (кого́ / что во что) *initiate (smb. / smth. in smth.)*
   2) *devote*
   3) *dedicate*

посели́ться *see* **сели́ться**

C **посёлок** *(gen.* посёлка*) settlement*

посла́ть *see* **посыла́ть**

A **по́сле**
   1) *(adv.) later*

2) *(prep. + gen.) after*

^A после́дний

    1) *last, latter*

    2) *new, latest*

после́довать *see* сле́довать

^C послеза́втра *the day after tomorrow*

послужи́ть *see* служи́ть

послу́шать *see* слу́шать

посме́ть *see* сметь

посмотре́ть *see* смотре́ть

посове́товать *see* сове́товать

поспеши́ть *see* спеши́ть

поспо́рить *see* спо́рить

^B посреди́

    1) *(prep. + gen.) in the middle of*

    2) *(adv.) in the middle*

поссо́риться *see* ссо́риться

поста́вить *see* ста́вить

постара́ться *see* стара́ться

^C посте́ль *(f.) bed*

^B постепе́нный (постепе́нен, постепе́нна) *gradual*

^A постоя́нный *constant*

^B постоя́ть (постою́, постои́т, постоя́т) *(pf.) stand (for a while)*

    постои́(те)! = *wait a bit!*

пострада́ть *see* страда́ть

постро́ить *see* стро́ить

^A поступа́ть / поступи́ть (поступлю́, посту́пит, посту́пят)

    1) *act*

    2) (во что *or* на что) *join (smth.), enter (smth.)*

    3) *(only in the 3rd pers.) be forthcoming, be received*

поступи́ть *see* поступа́ть

^B посту́пок *(gen.* посту́пка*) action, act, conduct*

^C посу́да *china, plates and dishes, table ware*

посчита́ться *see* счита́ться

^A посыла́ть / посла́ть (пошлю́, пошлёт, пошлю́т) *send*

118

^C **посы́лка** *(gen. pl.* посы́лок*)*
    1) *sending*
    2) *parcel*
^B **пот** (в поту́) *sweat*
  потемне́ть *see* **темне́ть**
  потерпе́ть *see* **терпе́ть**
  потеря́ть *see* **теря́ть**
^C **пото́к**
    1) *stream, torrent, flow, current*
    2) *production line*
^B **потоло́к** *(gen.* потолка́*)* *ceiling*
^A **пото́м** *then, afterwards*
^A **потому́ что** *because*
  потону́ть *see* **тону́ть**
  поторопи́ться *see* **торопи́ться**
  потре́бовать *see* **тре́бовать**
  потяну́ться *see* **тяну́ться**
  похвали́ть *see* **хвали́ть**
^B **похо́д**
    1) *campaign*
    2) *trip, tour, walking tour*
^A **похо́жий** (похо́ж, похо́жа)
    (на кого́ / что) *resembling (smb. / smth.)*
  поцелова́ть *see* **целова́ть**
^B **поцелу́й** *kiss*
^A **почему́** *why*
    почему́-то = *for some reason*
^C **почётный**
    1) *honorary, of honour*
    2) *honourable*
  почи́стить *see* **чи́стить**
^B **по́чта**
    1) *post*
    2) *mail*
    3) *post-office*
^A **почти́** *almost, nearly*
  пошевели́ть *see* **шевели́ть**
  пошевельну́ть *see* **шевели́ть**

пошути́ть *see* шути́ть

[В] поэ́т *poet*

[А] поэ́тому *therefore*

появи́ться *see* появля́ться

[А] появля́ться / появи́ться (появлю́сь, поя́вится, поя́вятся) *appear*

[С] по́яс *(pl.* пояса́*)*
1) *belt, girdle*
2) *waist*

[А] пра́вда *truth*
пра́вда? = *isn't it?*

[В] пра́вило *rule*

[А] пра́вильный (пра́вилен, пра́вильна)
right, true, correct

[В] прави́тельство *government*

[С] правле́ние
1) *government*
2) *board of administration, board of directors*

[А] пра́во *(pl. E)*
1) *right*
2) *law*

[А] пра́вый (прав, права́, пра́во)
1) *(only the attributive forms) right, righthand*
2) *right*
он прав = *he is right*

[А] пра́здник *holiday, a festive occasion*

[С] пра́ктика *practice*

преврати́ть *see* превраща́ть

[С] превраща́ть / преврати́ть (превращу́, преврати́т, превратя́т)
(кого́ / что во что) *turn (smb. / smth. into smth.)*

[А] предлага́ть / предложи́ть (предложу́, предло́жит, предло́жат)
1) *propose, suggest*
2) *offer*

[В] предложе́ние
1) *suggestion, proposal*
2) *proposal, offer of marriage*

3) *sentence*

предложи́ть *see* **предлага́ть**

A **предме́т**

    1) *object*

    2) *subject, topic*

B **предприя́тие** *undertaking, enterprise*

B **председа́тель** *(m.) chairman*

C **представи́тель** *(m.) representative*

предста́вить *see* **представля́ть**

B **представле́ние**

    1) *presentation*

    2) *performance*

    3) *idea, notion*

A **представля́ть / предста́вить** (предста́влю, предста́вит, предста́вят)

    1) *present, offer*

    2) *represent*

    3) *introduce*

    предста́вить себе́ = *imagine, conceive*

B **предстоя́ть** *(only in the 3rd pers.:* предстои́т, предстоя́т*) (ipf.)*

    (кому́ / чему́) нам предстои́т *we are faced with*

A **пре́жде**

    1) *(adv.) before, formerly*

    2) *(prep. + gen.) before*

    пре́жде всего́ = *first of all, above all*

    пре́жде чем говори́ть, поду́май = *think before you speak*

A **пре́жний** *previous, former*

B **презира́ть / презре́ть** (презрю́, презри́т, презря́т) *despise*

презре́ть *see* **презира́ть**

A **прекра́сный** (прекра́сен, прекра́сна) *beautiful, fine*

прекрати́ть *see* **прекраща́ть**

C **прекраща́ть / прекрати́ть** (прекращу́, прекрати́т, прекратя́т) *stop*

C **пре́лесть** *(f.) charm, fascination*

^A **при** *(prep. + the prepositional case)*

    1) *attached to*

    2) *in the presence of*

    3) *by, about, on, with*

    при Петре́ Пе́рвом = *under Peter the First*

  приба́вить *see* **прибавля́ть**

^A **прибавля́ть / приба́вить** (приба́влю, приба́вит, приба́вят) *add*

    приба́вить ша́гу = *quicken one's steps*

^A **прибега́ть / прибежа́ть** (прибегу́, прибежи́т, прибегу́т)

    1) *come running*

    2) (к кому́ / чему́) *run up (to smb. / smth.)*

  прибежа́ть *see* **прибега́ть**

^A **приближа́ться / прибли́зиться** (прибли́жусь, прибли́зится, прибли́зятся) *approach*

  прибли́зиться *see* **приближа́ться**

^B **прибо́р** *instrument, device, apparatus*

^C **прибыва́ть / прибы́ть** (прибу́ду, прибу́дет, прибу́дут; при́был, прибыла́, при́было, при́были)

    1) *arrive*

    2) *(only in the 3rd pers.) increase, grow*

  прибы́ть *see* **прибыва́ть**

  привезти́ *see* **привози́ть**

  привести́ *see* **приводи́ть**

^B **приве́т** *regards*

^B **приводи́ть** (привожу́, приво́дит, приво́дят) / **привести́** (приведу́, приведёт, приведу́т; привёл, привела́, привело́, привели́)

    1) *bring*

    2) *adduce, cite*

^B **привози́ть** (привожу́, приво́зит, приво́зят) / **привезти́** (привезу́, привезёт, привезу́т; привёз, привезла́, привезло́, привезли́)

    (кому́ что) *bring (smth. to smb.)*

^A **привыка́ть / привы́кнуть** (привы́кну, привы́кнет, привы́кнут; привы́к, привы́кла, привы́кло, привы́кли) (к кому́ / чему́) *get accustomed (to smb. | smth.)*

привы́кнуть *see* привыка́ть

^В привы́чка *(gen. pl.* привы́чек*) habit*

привяза́ть *see* привя́зывать

^С привя́зывать / привяза́ть (привяжу́, привя́жет, привя́жут)

(кого́ / что к кому́ / чему́)

1) *tie (smb. | smth. to smb. | smth.)*

2) *attach (smb. | smth. to smb. | smth.)*

пригласи́ть *see* приглаша́ть

^А приглаша́ть / пригласи́ть (приглашу́, пригласи́т, приглася́т) *invite*

приготóвить *see* приготовля́ть

^В приготовля́ть / приготóвить (приготóвлю, приготóвит, приготóвят) *prepare*

пригрози́ть *see* грози́ть

приду́мать *see* приду́мывать

^В приду́мывать / приду́мать *think of, devise, invent*

^С приéзд *arrival*

^А приезжа́ть / приéхать (приéду, приéдет, приéдут) *arrive, come (by some means of transport)*

^С приём

1) *receiving, reception*

2) *admittance*

приéхать *see* приезжа́ть

прижа́ть *see* прижима́ть

^С прижима́ть / прижа́ть (прижму́, прижмёт, прижму́т)

(кого́ / что к чему́) *press (smb. | smth. to smth.)*

^В признава́ть (признаю́, признаёт, признаю́т; признава́й) / призна́ть

1) *recognize*

2) *admit*

3) (когó / что кем / чем) *consider (smb. | smth. (to be) smb. | smth.)*

призна́ть *see* признава́ть

прийти́ *see* приходи́ть

прийти́сь *see* приходи́ться

^в **прика́з** *order, command*

приказа́ть *see* **прика́зывать**

^в **прика́зывать** / **приказа́ть** (прикажу́, прика́жет, прика́жут)

(кому́ / чему́) *(+ inf.) order (smb. / smth.) (to do smth.)*

^с **прилета́ть** / **прилете́ть** (прилечу́, прилети́т, прилетя́т) *come flying*

прилете́ть *see* **прилета́ть**

^А **приме́р** *example*

^в **принадлежа́ть** (принадлежу́, принадлежи́т, принадлежа́т) *(ipf.)*

1) (кому́ / чему́) *belong (to smb. / smth.)*

2) (к кому́ / чему́) *belong (under smb., to smb.'s staff, etc., to smth.)*

принести́ *see* **приноси́ть**

^А **принима́ть** / **приня́ть** (приму́, при́мет, при́мут; при́нял, приняла́, при́няло, при́няли)

1) *accept*

2) *take*

3) *admit*

4) *receive*

5) *pass, approve*

принима́ть уча́стие в рабо́те = *take part in the work*

принима́ть за пра́вило = *make it a rule*

принима́ть во внима́ние = *take into account*

^А **приноси́ть** (приношу́, прино́сит, прино́сят) / **принести́** (принесу́, принесёт, принесу́т; принёс, принесла́, принесло́, принесли́) *bring, fetch*

^с **при́нцип** *principle*

приня́ть *see* **принима́ть**

^А **приро́да** *nature*

присла́ть *see* **присыла́ть**

прислу́шаться *see* **прислу́шиваться**

^с **прислу́шиваться** / **прислу́шаться**

(к кому́ / чему́) *listen (to smb. / smth.)*

^C **прису́тствовать** (прису́тствую, прису́тствует, прису́тствуют) *(ipf.)* be present

^B **присыла́ть / присла́ть** (пришлю́, пришлёт, пришлю́т)

    1) (что кому́) *send (smth. to smb.)*

    2) (кого́ за чем) *send (smb. for, after, smth.)*

^A **приходи́ть** (прихожу́, прихо́дит, прихо́дят) / **прийти́** (приду́, придёт, приду́т; пришёл, пришла́, пришло́, пришли́) *come, arrive*

^A **приходи́ться** (прихожу́сь, прихо́дится, прихо́дятся) / **прийти́сь** (приду́сь, придётся, приду́тся; пришёлся, пришла́сь, пришло́сь, пришли́сь)

    1) *fit*

    2) *(impers., кому́) have to*

причеса́ться *see* **причёсываться**

^C **причёсываться / причеса́ться** (причешу́сь, причёшется, причёшутся) *do one's hair*

^A **причи́на** *cause, reason*

^B **прия́тель** *(m.) friend*

^A **прия́тный** (прия́тен, прия́тна) *pleasant, agreeable*

^A **про** *(prep. + acc.)*

    1) *about*

    2) *for*

    говори́ть про друзе́й = *talk about one's friends*

    э́то не про нас = *this is not for us*

    ду́мать про себя́ = *think to oneself*

^B **пробега́ть / пробежа́ть** (пробегу́, пробежи́т, пробегу́т)

    1) *(no object) run by*

    2) (что) *run, cover (smth.) (a distance)*

    3) (ми́мо кого́ / чего́) *run (past smb. / smth.)*

    3) (че́рез что) *run (through, along, smth.)*

    5) (чем по чему́) *run (smth. over smth.)*

пробежа́ть *see* **пробега́ть**

проби́ть *see* **бить**

^A **про́бовать** (про́бую, про́бует, про́буют), **ис-, по-**

    1) *(pf. ис-, по-) try, test*

2) (*pf.* по-) *taste*

3) (*pf.* по-) *attempt*

пробуди́ть *see* **буди́ть**

прове́рить *see* **проверя́ть**

^В **проверя́ть** / **прове́рить** (прове́рю, прове́рит, прове́рят) *verify, check, test*

провести́ *see* **проводи́ть**[1]

^А **проводи́ть**[1] (провожу́, прово́дит, прово́дят) / **провести́** (проведу́, проведёт, проведу́т; провёл, провела́, провело́, провели́)

1) *take, lead*

2) *draw*

3) *build, install*

4) *spend, pass*

проводи́ть[2] *see* **провожа́ть**

^А **провожа́ть** / **проводи́ть** (провожу́, прово́дит, прово́дят) *accompany, see off*

^С **програ́мма** *programme*

^С **прогу́лка** (*gen. pl.* прогу́лок)

1) *walk, stroll*

2) *drive, ride, row, sail*

^В **продава́ть** (продаю́, продаёт, продаю́т; продава́й) / **прода́ть** (прода́м, прода́шь, прода́ст, продади́м, продади́те, продаду́т; прода́й; про́дал, продала́, про́дало, про́дали) *sell*

^С **продавщи́ца** *seller, saleswoman, shop assistant*

прода́ть *see* **продава́ть**

^А **продолжа́ть** (*ipf.*) *continue*

^С **проду́кт**

1) *product, produce*

2) (*only pl.*) *provisions, victuals*

^С **проезжа́ть** / **прое́хать** (прое́ду, прое́дет, прое́дут)

1) (что *or* ми́мо чего́) *drive (past smth.)*

2) *do, make, cover (a distance)*

^С **прое́кт** *project, design, scheme, draft*

прое́хать *see* **проезжа́ть**

^С **прожива́ть** / **прожи́ть** (проживу́, проживёт, про-

живу́т; про́жил, прожила́, про́жило, про́жили)

1) *live*

2) *spend (on necessities)*

прожи́ть *see* прожива́ть

^С прозра́чный (прозра́чен, прозра́чна)

1) *transparent*

2) *obvious*

проигра́ть *see* проигрывать

^С прои́грывать / проигра́ть

(что кому́) *lose (smth. to smb.)*

проигра́ть в чьём-нибудь мне́нии = проигра́ть в чьём-нибудь глаза́х = *sink in smb.'s estimation*

произвести́ *see* производи́ть

^В производи́ть (произвожу́, произво́дит, произво́дят) / произвести́ (произведу́, произведёт, произведу́т; произвёл, произвела́, произвело́, произвели́) *make, produce*

^В произво́дство *production, manufacture*

произнести́ *see* произноси́ть

^С произноси́ть (произношу́, произно́сит, произно́сят) / произнести́ (произнесу́, произнесёт, произнесу́т; произнёс, произнесла́, произнесло́, произнесли́)

1) *pronounce*

2) *utter*

произойти́ *see* происходи́ть

^А происходи́ть *(only in the 3rd pers.:* происхо́дит, происхо́дят) / произойти́ *(only in the 3rd pers.:* произойдёт, произойду́т; произошёл, произошла́, произошло́, произошли́) *happen, occur, take place*

пройти́ *see* проходи́ть

^С прокля́тый *cursed, damned*

прокорми́ть *see* корми́ть

^С пролета́ть / пролете́ть (пролечу́, пролети́т, пролетя́т)

1) *fly past*
2) *fly (a distance)*
3) *fly by (ab. time)*

пролете́ть *see* **пролета́ть**

C **промы́шленность** *(f.) industry*

A **пропада́ть / пропа́сть** (пропаду́, пропадёт, пропаду́т; пропа́л, пропа́ла, пропа́ло, пропа́ли)
1) *be missing, be lost*
2) *(only in the 3rd pers.) be wasted*

пропа́сть *see* **пропада́ть**

пропе́ть *see* **петь**

C **пропуска́ть / пропусти́ть** (пропущу́, пропу́стит, пропу́стят)
1) *let through*
2) *let pass*
3) *omit*
4) *miss*

пропусти́ть *see* **пропуска́ть**

A **проси́ть** (прошу́, про́сит, про́сят), **по-** *ask, beg*

прослу́шать *see* **слу́шать**

просну́ться *see* **просыпа́ться**

B **проспе́кт** *avenue*

прости́ть *see* **проща́ть**

прости́ться *see* **проща́ться**

A **про́сто** *simply*

A **просто́й** (прост, проста́, про́сто, про́сты; про́ще)
1) *simple, easy*
2) *common, plain, ordinary*
3) *mere*

C **просто́рный** (просто́рен, просто́рна) *spacious*

C **простра́нство** *space*

простуди́ться *see* **просту́живаться**

C **просту́живаться / простуди́ться** (простужу́сь, просту́дится, просту́дятся) *catch a cold*

A **просыпа́ться / просну́ться** (просну́сь, проснётся, просну́тся) *wake up*

B **про́сьба** *request*

A **про́тив** *(prep. + gen.)*

1) *opposite*

2) *against*

стоя́ть про́тив зда́ния = *stand opposite a building*

боро́ться про́тив врага́ = *fight against the enemy*

C **проти́вный** (проти́вен, проти́вна)

  1) *opposite*

  2) *nasty, offensive*

B **протя́гивать / протяну́ть** (протяну́, протя́нет, протя́нут)

  1) *stretch*

  2) *stretch out, reach out*

  3) *draw (sound)*

протяну́ть *see* **протя́гивать**

A **профе́ссия** *occupation, profession, trade*

B **профе́ссор** *(pl.* профессора́*) professor*

C **прохла́дный** (прохла́ден, прохла́дна) *fresh, cool*

A **проходи́ть** (прохожу́, прохо́дит, прохо́дят) / **пройти́** (пройду́, пройдёт, пройду́т; прошёл, прошла́, прошло́, прошли́)

  1) *pass, go, cross*

  2) (что *or* ми́мо чего́) *go (past smth.)*

  3) *pass, elapse*

  4) *be over*

  5) *study*

B **прохо́жий** *passer-by*

C **проце́сс**

  1) *process*

  2) *trial, suit*

прочéсть *see* **читáть**

B **про́чий** *other*

и про́чее (и пр.) = *etcetera*

мéжду про́чим = *by the way*

прочита́ть *see* **чита́ть**

C **про́чный** (про́чен, прочна́, про́чно, про́чны)

  1) *solid, firm*

  2) *stable, durable*

^C **прошепта́ть** (прошепчу́, проше́пчет, проше́пчут) *(pf.)* whisper

^A **про́шлый** *past, last*

^A **проща́ть** / **прости́ть** (прощу́, прости́т, простя́т) *forgive*

    проща́й(те)! = *good-bye!*

^B **проща́ться** / **прости́ться** (прощу́сь, прости́тся, простя́тся)

    (с кем / чем) *take leave (of smb. / smth.)*

  про́ще *see* **просто́й**

^B **пры́гать** / **пры́гнуть** (пры́гну, пры́гнет, пры́гнут) *spring, jump, leap*

  пры́гнуть *see* **пры́гать**

^A **пря́мо**

    1) *straight*

    2) *frankly, bluntly*

^B **прямо́й** (прям, пряма́, пря́мо)

    1) *straight, erect*

    2) *through*

    3) *direct*

    4) *straightforward*

^A **пря́тать** (пря́чу, пря́чет, пря́чут), **с-** *hide, conceal*

^A **пти́ца** *bird*

^B **пу́блика** *public, audience*

^A **пуга́ться, ис-** *be frightened*

^C **пу́говица** *button*

^A **пуска́ть** / **пусти́ть** (пущу́, пу́стит, пу́стят)

    1) *set free*

    2) *let go*

    3) *start, put in action*

  пусти́ть *see* **пуска́ть**

^A **пусто́й** (пуст, пуста́, пу́сто)

    1) *empty*

    2) *idle, shallow*

^A **пусть** *let*

    пусть он придёт за́втра = *let him come to-morrow*

^B **пустя́к** *(E)* *trifle*

^C **путешéствие** *journey, voyage, trip*

^A **путь** *(m.)* *(sg. gen., dat., the prepositional case*
пути́, *instr.* путём, *pl. nom.* пути́, *gen.* путéй,
dat. путя́м)
1) *way*
2) *journey*
3) *means*

^B **пыль** *(f.)* (в пыли́) *dust*

^B **пьéса**
1) *play*
2) *(short) piece of music*

^B **пья́ный** (пьян, пьяна́, пья́но) *drunk, intoxicated*

^C **пя́теро** *(gen.* пятеры́х*) five*

пятисóт *see* **пятьсóт**

пятистáм *see* **пятьсóт**

пятистáх *see* **пятьсóт**

^A **пятнáдцать** *(gen.* пятнáдцати*) fifteen*

^A **пя́тница** *Friday*

^B **пятнó** *(pl. nom.* пя́тна, *gen.* пя́тен*) spot*

^A **пя́тый** *fifth*

^A **пять** *(gen.* пяти́*) five*

^A **пятьдеся́т** *(gen., dat., the prepositional case*
пяти́десяти, *instr.* пятью́десятью*) fifty*

^A **пятьсóт** *(gen.* пятисóт, *dat.* пятистáм, *instr.*
пятьюстáми, *the prepositional case* пятистáх*)*
five hundred

пятьюстáми *see* **пятьсóт**

Р

^A **рабóта** *work*

^A **рабóтать** *(ipf.)*
1) *work*
2) *be open*

^B **рабóтник**
1) *worker*
2) *(preceded by an attributive adj. or followed*
by the gen. of word(s) indicating field of work)
нау́чный рабóтник *scientist*

3) *farm-hand*

^B **рабо́тница**

    1) *worker (ab. woman)*

    2) *(preceded by an attributive adj. or followed by the gen. of word(s) indicating field of work)* дома́шняя рабо́тница *(domestic) servant*

    3) *working-class woman*

^A **рабо́чий**

    1) *worker's, working*

    2) *work, working*

    3) *(used substantively) worker, labourer*

^A **равно́** *alike*

    мне всё равно́ = *it's all the same to me*

^B **равноду́шный** (равноду́шен, равноду́шна) *indifferent*

^B **ра́вный** (ра́вен, равна́) *equal*

^A **рад** (ра́да) *(only the predicative forms are used)* (кому́ / чему́) *glad (of, about, because of, smb. / smth.)*

    рад стара́ться! = *willingly! with pleasure!*

^B **ра́ди** *(prep. + gen.) for the sake of*

^A **ра́дио** *(indeclinable n.) radio, wireless*

^A **ра́доваться** (ра́дуюсь, ра́дуется, ра́дуются), об- (кому́ / чему́) *be pleased (with smb. / smth.), be happy (about smb. / smth.)*

^A **ра́дость** *(f.) gladness, joy*

^A **раз** *(pl. E, gen. pl. раз) time*

    как раз вчера́ = *only yesterday*

    э́то как раз то, что я сказа́л = *that is just what I said*

    не раз = *several times*

    ни ра́зу не = *never*

    в са́мый раз = *in due time*

    раз-два-три = *1-2-3 (counting)*

^B **раз** *if*

^C **разбира́ться / разобра́ться** (разберу́сь, разберётся, разберу́тся; разобра́лся, разобрала́сь, разобра́лось, разобра́ли́сь)

разби́ть *see* **бить**

1) *make one's arrangements, unpack*

2) (в чём) *examine (smth.), understand (smth.)*

разбуди́ть *see* **буди́ть**

A **ра́зве**

1) *really*

2) *(at the beginning of an interrogative sentence) not translated*

ра́зве он прие́хал? = *has he come?*

B **разви́тие** *development*

разгляде́ть *see* **разгля́дывать**

C **разгля́дывать** / **разгляде́ть** (разгляжу́, разгляди́т, разглядя́т) *view, examine*

A **разгова́ривать** *(ipf.)*

(с кем) *talk, (to, with, smb.), converse (with smb.)*

A **разгово́р** *talk, conversation*

де́лайте без разгово́ров = *do as you are told*

A **раздава́ться** *(only in the 3rd pers.:* раздаётся, раздаю́тся) / **разда́ться** *(only in the 3rd pers.:* разда́стся, раздаду́тся; разда́лся, раздала́сь, разда́лось, разда́ли́сь) *be heard, sound, resound*

разда́ться *see* **раздава́ться**

B **раздева́ться** / **разде́ться** (разде́нусь, разде́нется, разде́нутся)

1) *undress*

2) *take off one's coat*

раздели́ть *see* **дели́ть**

разде́ться *see* **раздева́ться**

A **разли́чный** (разли́чен, разли́чна)

1) *different*

2) *diverse, various*

C **разноцве́тный** *many-coloured, motley, variegated*

A **ра́зный** *different, diverse, various*

разобра́ться *see* **разбира́ться**

разойти́сь *see* **расходи́ться**

разре́зать *see* **ре́зать**

A **разреша́ть** / **разреши́ть** (разрешу́, разреши́т, разреша́т)

1) *allow, permit*

2) *solve*

разреши́ть *see* **разреша́ть**

ᴮ **разруша́ть / разру́шить** (разру́шу, разру́шит, разру́шат) *destroy, wreck*

разру́шить *see* **разруша́ть**

ᴮ **разуме́ться** *(ipf.) (only in the 3rd pers. sg.:* разуме́ется) *be understood*

разуме́ется само́ собо́й = *it goes without saying*

ᴬ **райо́н**

1) *region, area*

2) *district*

ᶜ **раке́та** *rocket*

ᶜ **ра́неный** *injured, wounded*

ᶜ **ра́нить** (ра́ню, ра́нит, ра́нят) *(ipf. / pf.) injure, wound*

ᴬ **ра́нний** *early*

ᴬ **ра́но** *(comp.* ра́ньше) *early*

ра́ньше *see* **ра́но**

ᶜ **раскрыва́ть / раскры́ть** (раскро́ю, раскро́ет, раскро́ют)

1) *open, put up*

2) *reveal, disclose*

раскры́ть *see* **раскрыва́ть**

ᴮ **располо́женный**

1) (к чему́ + *inf.) inclined (to do smth.)*

2) *situated*

ᶜ **расеве́т** *dawn*

рассерди́ться *see* **серди́ться**

ᴬ **расска́з**

1) *account*

2) *story, tale*

рассказа́ть *see* **расска́зывать**

ᴬ **расска́зывать / рассказа́ть** (расскажу́, расска́жет, расска́жут) *tell*

ᴮ **рассма́тривать / рассмотре́ть** (рассмотрю́, рассмо́трит, рассмо́трят) *consider, examine*

ᴮ **рассмея́ться** (рассмею́сь, рассмеётся, рассме-
ю́тся) *(pf.) burst out laughing*

рассмотре́ть *see* **рассма́тривать**

ᴮ **расстава́ться** (расстаю́сь, расстаётся, расстаю́т-
ся) / **расста́ться** (расста́нусь, расста́нется,
расста́нутся)
(с кем / чем) *part (with smb. / smth.)*

расста́ться *see* **расстава́ться**

ᶜ **расстёгивать** / **расстегну́ть** (расстегну́, расстег-
нёт, расстегну́т) *undo, unfasten, unbutton*

расстегну́ть *see* **расстёгивать**

ᶜ **расстоя́ние** *distance*

раста́ять *see* **та́ять**

ᶜ **расте́ние** *plant*

ᴮ **расте́рянный**
1) *lost*
2) *confused, embarrassed, perplexed*

ᴬ **расти́** (расту́, растёт, расту́т; рос, росла́, росло́,
росли́), **вы-**
1) *grow*
2) *grow up*

ᶜ **расходи́ться** (расхожу́сь, расхо́дится, расхо́дят-
ся) / **разойти́сь** (разойду́сь, разойдётся, ра-
зойду́тся; разошёлся, разошла́сь, разошло́сь,
разошли́сь)
1) *(only in the 3rd pers.) go away from one
another, disperse*
2) *(only in the 3rd pers.) be sold out*
3) *(only in the 3rd pers.) dissolve*
4) (с кем) *get divorced (from smb.)*
5) (с кем / чем в чём) *differ (from smb. / smth.
in smth.)*

ᶜ **расчёт**
1) *calculation, computation*
2) *settling*
3) *detachment*
дать расчёт кому́-нибудь = *discharge smb.*

нет расчёта де́лать э́то = *it is not worth while*

C **рвать** (рву, рвёт, рвут; рвал, рвала́, рва́ло, рва́ли) *(ipf.)*
   1) *tear off, tear to pieces, pull out*
   2) *pick*
   3) *blow up*
   4) *break (relations)*

A **ребёнок** *(gen. sg.* ребёнка, *pl. nom.* ребя́та, *gen.* ребя́т; *note* де́ти *(which see) is in most cases used instead of the pl. forms of* ребёнок*)*
   1) *child*
   2) *(only pl.) (in addressing persons)* "lads", "old fellows", "dear friends"

   ребя́та *see* **ребёнок**

B **револю́ция** *revolution*

C **реда́кция**
   1) *editorial staff, editorial office*
   2) *editorship*
   3) *wording*

B **ре́дкий** (ре́док, редка́, ре́дко; ре́же)
   1) *thin, sparse, thinly growing*
   2) *rare*

   ре́же *see* **ре́дкий**

C **ре́зать** (ре́жу, ре́жет, ре́жут), за-, раз-
   1) *(only ipf.) cut*
   2) *(pf.* раз-*) slit, section*
   3) *(pf.* за-*) kill, slaughter*

A **ре́зкий** (ре́зок, резка́, ре́зко; ре́зче)
   1) *abrupt*
   2) *sharp, harsh, shrill*

A **результа́т** *result*

   ре́зче *see* **ре́зкий**

A **река́** *(sg. acc.* ре́ку́, *gen.* реки́, *pl. nom.* ре́ки *dat.* река́м*) river*

C **ремо́нт** *repair(s)*

C **ресни́ца** *eyelash*

C **респу́блика** *republic*

A **рестора́н** *restaurant*

^A **речь** *(f.) (gen. pl.* речéй*) speech*
    речь идёт о том, что... *= the question is that*
^A **решáть / решить** (решý, решит, решáт)
    1) *decide*
    2) *solve*
^A **решительный** (решителен, решительна)
    1) *firm, resolute*
    2) *absolute, decided*
    3) *decisive*
  решить *see* **решáть**
^B **рисовáть** (рисýю, рисýет, рисýют), **на-** *draw, paint*
^B **рисýнок** *(gen.* рисýнка*) drawing*
^B **рóбкий** (рóбок, робкá, рóбко; рóбче) *shy, timid*
  рóбче *see* **рóбкий**
^A **рóвный** (рóвен, ровнá, рóвно)
    1) *flat, even, level*
    2) *even, equal, equable*
^C **род** *(pl. E)*
    1) (в, на, родý) *family, kin*
    2) (в, на, родý) *birth, origin*
    3) *(only sg.) sort, kind*
    4) *gender*
^B **рóдина** *native land*
^A **родители** *(only pl.) (gen.* родителей*) parents*
  родиться *see* **рождáться**
^A **роднóй**
    1) *own*
    2) *native*
    3) *(used substantively, only pl.) relatives*
    роднóй *(in addressing a person) = my dear*
^C **рóдственник** *relative, relation*
^A **рождáться / родиться** (рожýсь, родится, родятся; родился, родилáсь, родилóсь, родились) *be born*
^B **рождéние** *birth*
^C **рóза** *rose*
^B **рóзовый** *pink*
^B **роль** *(f.) (gen. pl.* ролéй*) role, part*

^C **рома́н** *novel*
^C **роня́ть / урони́ть** (уроню́, уро́нит, уро́нят) *drop, let fall*
^C **Росси́я** *Russia*
^A **рост**
    1) *growth, increase*
    2) *height, stature*
^A **рот** *(gen.* рта; во рту*) mouth*
^A **руба́шка** *(gen. pl.* руба́шек*) shirt, chemise*
^A **рубль** *(gen.* рубля́*) rouble*
^B **руга́ть, вы-, об-, от-** *scold*
^C **ружьё** *(pl. nom.* ру́жья *gen.* ру́жей*) gun*
^A **рука́** *(sg. acc.* ру́ку, *gen.* руки́, *pl. nom.* ру́ки, *dat.* рука́м*)*
    1) *hand*
    2) *arm*
    име́ть золоты́е ру́ки = *be master of one's craft*
    брать себя́ в ру́ки = *pull oneself together*
    из пе́рвых рук = *from good authority*
    на ско́рую ру́ку = *off-hand*
    под руко́й = *(near) at hand*
    свобо́да рук = *freedom of action*
^B **рука́в** *(E; pl.* рукава́*)*
    1) *sleeve*
    2) *branch, arm*
^B **руководи́тель** *(m.) leader*
^B **руководи́ть** (руковожу́, руководи́т, руководя́т) *(ipf.)*
    (кем / чем) *lead (smb. | smth.)*
^A **ру́сский** *Russian*
^B **руче́й** *(gen.* ручья́*) brook, stream*
^B **ру́чка** *(gen. pl.* ру́чек*)*
    1) *small hand*
    2) *handle, knob*
    3) *penholder*
    4) *arm (of a chair)*
    автомати́ческая ру́чка = авторучка = *fountain-pen*

^A **ры́ба** *fish*

ни ры́ба ни мя́со = *neither flesh nor fowl (nor good red herring)*

^B **ры́жий** (рыж, рыжа́, ры́же)

1) *red, ginger*
2) *chestnut*
3) *red-haired*

^C **ры́нок** *(gen.* ры́нка) *market(place)*

^A **ряд** (в ряду́ / в ря́де; *pl.* E)

1) (в ряду́) *row, line*
2) (в ря́де) *series*

^A **ря́дом** *near*

он шёл ря́дом с ней = *he walked beside her*

C

^A **с** (со) *(prep.* + *gen., instr. or acc.)*

(+ *gen.) from*
(+ *instr.) with, and*
(+ *acc.) about, the size of*
верну́ться с рабо́ты = *return from work*
говори́ть с друзья́ми = *talk with one's friends*
оте́ц с ма́терью = *father and mother*
с год = *about a year*

^A **сад** (в саду́; *pl.* E) *garden*

^A **сади́ться** (сажу́сь, сади́тся, садя́тся) / **сесть** (ся́ду, ся́дет, ся́дут; сел, се́ла, се́ло, се́ли)

1) *sit down*
2) *get on (bus, etc.)*
3) *alight, settle*
4) *set (ab. the sun)*

^B **сажа́ть** / **посади́ть** (посажу́, поса́дит, поса́дят)

1) *plant*
2) *seat*

^A **сам** *(gen.* самого́; *f.* сама́, *gen.* само́й; *n.* само́, *gen.* самого́; *pl.* са́ми, *gen.* сами́х) *myself, yourself, himself, herself, itself, ourselves, yourselves, themselves*

^C **самова́р** *samovar*

^B **самолёт** *aeroplane*

^B **самостоя́тельный** (самостоя́телен, самостоя́тельна) *independent*

^A **са́мый**
   1) *the very*
   2) *the most*
   в са́мом де́ле = *indeed ? really?*
   на са́мом де́ле = *actually*
   на са́мом берегу́ = *on the very bank*
   с са́мого нача́ла = *from the very beginning*
   тот (же) са́мый челове́к = *just the man*

^C **са́ни** *(only pl.) (gen.* сане́й*) sledge, sleigh*

^A **сапо́г** *(E) (gen. pl.* сапо́г*) (high) boot*

^C **сара́й**
   1) *shed*
   2) *barn*

^C **са́хар** *(gen.* са́хара / са́хару*) sugar*

^C **сбо́рник** *collection*

^C **сва́дьба** *(gen. pl.* сва́деб*) wedding*

^A **све́жий** (свеж, свежа́, свежо́, све́жи)
   1) *fresh*
   2) *cool*

^C **сверка́ть / сверкну́ть** *(only in the 3rd pers.:* сверкнёт, сверкну́т*) sparkle, twinkle, glitter, glare*
   сверкну́ть *see* **сверка́ть**

^A **све́рху**
   1) *from above*
   2) *on top*

^A **свет**
   1) *light*
   2) *world*

^A **свети́ть** (свечу́, све́тит, све́тят), **по-**
   1) *(only ipf.) shine*
   2) *(кому́ / чему́) light (smb. / smth.)*

^A **све́тлый** (све́тел, светла́, све́тло́, све́тлы) *light, bright*

^B **свеча́** *(pl. nom.* све́чи, *gen.* свече́й*)*

1) *candle*
2) *candle-power*

игра́ не сто́ит свеч = *the game is not worth the candle*

^A **свида́ние** *meeting, appointment, rendezvous*

до свида́ния! = *good-bye!*

^C **свисте́ть** (свищу́, свисти́т, свистя́т *or* сви́щет, сви́щут) / **сви́стнуть** (сви́стну, сви́стнет, сви́стнут) *whistle*

сви́стнуть *see* **свисте́ть**

^B **свобо́да** *freedom, liberty*

^A **свобо́дный** (свобо́ден, свобо́дна)
1) *free*
2) *vacant*
3) *spare*

^A **свой** (*gen.* своего́; *f.* своя́, *gen.* свое́й; *n.* своё, *gen.* своего́; *pl.* свои́, *gen.* свои́х)
1) *one's*
2) *my, your, his, her, its, our, their*
2) *(only pl.) one's people*

связа́ть *see* **свя́зывать**

^C **свя́зывать** / **связа́ть** (свяжу́, свя́жет, свя́жут)
1) *tie together*
2) *connect, link together*
3) *tie*

^A **связь** *(f.)* (в связи́)
1) *tie, bond*
2) *connection, relation*
3) *communication*

^C **свято́й** (свят, свята́, свя́то) *holy*

сгоре́ть *see* **горе́ть**

^B **сдава́ть** (сдаю́, сдаёт, сдаю́т; сдава́й) / **сдать** (сдам, сдашь, сдаст, сдади́м, сдади́те, сдаду́т; сдай; сдал, сдала́, сда́ло, сда́ли)
1) *pass, hand in, return*
2) *let, rent*
3) *reduce*
4) *pass (an examination)*

5) *be weakened*

сдать *see* сдава́ть

сде́лать *see* де́лать

сде́латься *see* де́латься

сдержа́ть *see* сде́рживать

B сде́рживать / сдержа́ть (сдержу́, сде́ржит, сде́ржат

    1) *hold in, hold back*

    2) *restrain, repress*

    3) *keep*

себе́ *see* себя́

A себя́ *(gen.* себя́, *dat., the prepositional case* себе́, *instr.* собо́й*)*

    1) *oneself*

    2) *myself, yourself, himself, herself, itself, ourselves, yourselves, themselves*

    сам по себе́ = *in itself, actually*

A се́вер *north*

A сего́дня *today*

    не сего́дня-за́втра = *very soon, one of these days*

C сего́дняшний *today's*

B седо́й (сед, седа́, се́до) *grey(-haired), grey(-bearded)*

A седьмо́й *seventh*

B сей *(gen. m. and n.* сего́, *gen. pl.* сих, *acc. f.* сию́*) this (now only used in stock phrases)*

    второ́го а́вгуста сего́ го́да = *on the 2nd August this year*

    до сих пор = *up to now, hitherto*

    сию́ мину́ту = *this very minute*

A сейча́с

    1) *right now*

    2) *presently, soon, at once*

    3) *a moment ago, this very moment*

C секрета́рь *(gen.* секретаря́*) secretary*

B секу́нда *second*

C сели́ться (селю́сь, сели́тся, селя́тся), по- *settle*

^B **село́** *(pl.* сёла*)* *village*

^C **се́льский**
1) *village*
2) *rural*
се́льское хозя́йство = *agriculture*

^C **сельскохозя́йственный** *agricultural*

^C **семе́йный**
1) *domestic, family*
2) *(having a) family*

^B **семна́дцать** *(gen.* семна́дцати*)* *seventeen*

^A **семь** *(gen.* семи́*)* *seven*

^A **семья́** *(pl. nom.* се́мьи, *gen.* семе́й, *dat.* се́мьям*)* *family*

^B **се́ни** *(only pl.)* *(gen.* сене́й*)* *(entrance-)hall*

^C **се́но** *hay*

^A **сентя́брь** *(gen.* сентября́*)* *September*

^C **серде́чный** (серде́чен, серде́чна)
1) *cordial, hearty*
2) *of the heart*

^A **серди́тый**
1) *angry, cross*
2) *hot-tempered*

^A **серди́ться** (сержу́сь, се́рдится, се́рдятся), **рас-** (на кого́ / что) *be angry (with smb. | smth.)*

^A **се́рдце** *(pl. nom.* сердца́, *gen.* серде́ц*)* *heart*

^C **серебро́** *silver*

^B **сере́бряный** *silver*

^C **середи́на** *middle, midst*

^A **се́рый** (сер, сера́, се́ро) *grey*

^A **серьёзный** (серьёзен, серьёзна) *serious, earnest, grave*

^A **сестра́** *(pl. nom.* сёстры, *gen.* сестёр, *dat.* сёстрам*)* *sister*
двою́родная сестра́ = *(first) cousin*

сесть *see* **сади́ться**

^B **сза́ди**
1) *(adv.)* *behind, from behind*
2) *(prep.* + *gen.)* *behind*

^C **Сиби́рь** *(f.)* Siberia

^C **сигна́л** signal

^A **сиде́ть** (сижу́, сиди́т, сидя́т) *(ipf.)* sit
вот где сиди́т он у меня́ = *he is always putting me to a lot of trouble*

^A **си́ла** strength, force
мне э́то не под си́лу = *it is too much for me*
собра́ться с си́лами = *regain one's strength*

^A **си́льный** (си́лён, сильна́, си́льно) strong, powerful

^A **си́ний** (синь, синя́, си́не, си́ни) *(dark) blue*

^C **систе́ма** system

сих *see* **сей**

^C **сия́ть** *(ipf.)* shine, beam

сказа́ть *see* **говори́ть**

^B **ска́зка** *(gen. pl.* ска́зок) tale, story

^A **скаме́йка** *(gen. pl.* скаме́ек) bench

^A **сквозь** *(prep. + acc.)* through

^C **скла́дывать / сложи́ть** (сложу́, сло́жит, сло́жат)
1) *put together*
2) *add*
3) *compose*
4) *fold up*

^B **скользи́ть** (скольжу́, скользи́т, скользя́т) / **скользну́ть** (скользну́, скользнёт, скользну́т) slip, slide

^C **ско́льзкий** (ско́льзок, скользка́, ско́льзко) slippery

скользну́ть *see* **скользи́ть**

^A **ско́лько** how much, how many
ско́лько вре́мени? = *how long? what time (is it)?*
ско́лько изве́стно = *as far as I know, for all I know*

^A **скоре́е**
1) *sooner*
2) *rather*
скоре́е всего́ = *most likely*
как мо́жно скоре́е = *as soon as possible*

^A **ско́рый** (скор, скора́, ско́ро)
   1) *quick, fast*
   2) *impatient*
   3) *near, forthcoming*
   на ско́рую ру́ку = *offhand*

^C **скрипе́ть** (скриплю́, скрипи́т, скрипя́т) / **скри́п-нуть** (скри́пну, скри́пнет, скри́пнут) *squeak, creak, crunch*
   скрипе́ть зуба́ми = *grit one's teeth*

^C **скри́пка** *(gen. pl.* скри́пок*) violin*

скри́пнуть *see* **скрипе́ть**

^C **скро́мный** (скро́мен, скромна́, скро́мно) *modest*

^C **скрыва́ть** / **скрыть** (скро́ю, скро́ет, скро́ют) *hide, conceal*

скрыть *see* **скрыва́ть**

^C **скуча́ть** *(ipf.)*
   1) *be bored*
   2) (по ком / чём *or* по кому́ / чему́ *or* о ком / чём) *miss (smb. / smth.), be longing (for smb. / smth.)*

^A **ску́чный** (ску́чен, скучна́, ску́чно, ску́чны́) *dull, boring, tedious*
   мне ску́чно = *I am bored*

ску́шать *see* **ку́шать**

^C **слабе́ть** (слабе́ю, слабе́ет, слабе́ют), **о-** *weaken*

^A **сла́бый** (слаб, слаба́, сла́бо, сла́бы́) *weak, faint, feeble*

^B **сла́ва** *glory, fame*
   сла́ва Бо́гу! = *thank God!*

^Б **сла́вный** (сла́вен, славна́, сла́вно)
   1) *glorious*
   2) *famous, renowned*
   сла́вный ма́лый = *nice fellow*

^C **сла́дкий** (сла́док, сладка́, сла́дко; сла́ще)
   1) *sweet*
   2) *sugary*

сла́ще *see* **сла́дкий**

^A **сле́ва** *to the left*

^C **слегка** *slightly, gently, somewhat*

^B **след** (в, на, слéде / следý; *pl. E*) *track, footprint, trace*

^A **следить** (слежý, следит, следят) *(ipf.)*
    (за кем / чем) 1) *follow (smb. / smth.) with one's eyes*
    2) *watch (smb. / smth.), have an eye (on smb. / smth.)*

^A **следовать** (слéдую, слéдует, слéдуют), **по-**
    1) (за кем / чем) *follow (smb. / smth.)*
    2) *(only ipf.)* (до чегó) *be bound (for smth.)*
    3) (комý / чемý) *follow (smb. / smth.), do as, behave like (smb. / smth.)*
    4) *follow (as a result)*
    5) *(only ipf.) (impers.,* комý / чемý*) ought to*
    как слéдует = *properly*

^A **слéдующий** *following, next*

^A **слезá** *(pl. nom.* слёзы, *gen.* слёз, *dat.* слезáм*) tear*
    слезáми гóрю не помóжешь = *it is no use crying over spilt milk*
    довести когó-нибудь до слёз = *make somebody cry*

^C **слезáть / слезть** (слéзу, слéзет, слéзут; слез, слéзла, слéзло, слéзли) *come down, get down, dismount, alight*
  слезть *see* **слезáть**

^C **слепóй** (слеп, слепá, слéпо) *blind*

^A **слишком** *too*

^A **слóвно**
    1) *like*
    2) *as if*

^A **слóво** *(pl. E)*
    1) *word*
    2) *speech, address*
    3) *remark*
  сложить *see* **склáдывать**

^A **слóжный** (слóжен, сложнá, слóжно) *complicated,*

complex, intricate

сломáть *see* **ломáть**

B **слýжба**
1) *service, work*
2) *(divine) service*

A **служи́ть** (служý, слýжит, слýжат), **по-**
1) (комý / чемý) *serve (smb. / smth.)*
2) (кем / чем) *serve (as smb. / smth.)*
3) (чем) *be (smth.)*

C **слух**
1) *hearing*
2) *ear*
3) *rumour, hearsay*

A **слýчай** *case*
несчáстный слýчай = *accident*

A **случáться / случи́ться** *(only in the 3rd pers.:* случи́тся, случáтся) *happen, occur*

случи́ться *see* **случáться**

A **слýшать, про-, по-**
1) *(only ipf.) listen to*
2) *obey*

A **слы́шать** (слы́шу, слы́шит, слы́шат), **у-**
1) *hear*
2) *learn*

A **слы́шный** (слы́шен, слышнá, слы́шно, слы́шны́) *audible*

A **смéлый** (смел, смелá, смéло) *bold, courageous*

B **смéна**
1) *changing*
2) *shift*

B **смерть** *(f.) death*

B **сметь** (смéю, смéет, смéют), **по-** *dare, make bold*

A **смех** *(gen.* смéха / смéху) *laughter*
смéху рáди = *just for fun*

смешáть *see* **мешáть**

B **смешнóй** (смешóн, смешнá, смешнó) *ridiculous, funny*

A **смея́ться** (смею́сь, смеётся, смею́тся) *(ipf.)*

(над кем / чем) *laugh (at smb. / smth.)*

^C **сми́рный** (сми́рён, смирна́, сми́рно) *quiet, mild*

^A **смотре́ть** (смотрю́, смо́трит, смо́трят), **по-**
    1) (на кого́ / что) *look (at smb. / smth.)*
    2) (во что) *look (in at smth.), look (out of smth.)*
    3) *see, watch*
    4) *(only ipf. and only the imperative forms) take care, look out*

  смочь *see* **мочь**

  смути́ться *see* **смуща́ться**

^C **смуща́ться / смути́ться** (смущу́сь, смути́тся, смутя́тся) *be confused, be embarrassed*

^B **смущённый** *confused, embarrassed*

^A **смысл** *sense, meaning*

^A **снача́ла**
    1) *at first, at the beginning*
    2) *all over again*

^A **снег** *(gen.* сне́га / сне́гу, *pl.* снега́)
    1) *snow*
    2) *(only pl.) masses of snow*
    снег идёт = *it is snowing*

^C **сни́зу** *from below*

^A **снима́ть / снять** (сниму́, сни́мет, сни́мут)
    1) *take away, take off*
    2) *photograph*
    3) *rent*

^C **сни́мок** *(gen.* сни́мка*) photograph*

^A **сно́ва** *anew, afresh, again*

  снять *see* **снима́ть**

  со *see* **с**

^A **соба́ка** *dog*

^A **собира́ть / собра́ть** (соберу́, соберёт, соберу́т; собра́л, собрала́, собра́ло, собра́ли)
    1) *gather*
    2) *collect*
    3) *assemble*

^A **собира́ться / собра́ться** (соберу́сь, соберётся, со-

беру́тся; собра́лся, собрала́сь, собрало́сь, собра́ли́сь)

1) *gather, assemble*
2) *intend*
3) *be going, be about*

собо́й *see* себя́

^C собо́р
1) *cathedral*
2) *(old) council, synod*

^A собра́ние
1) *meeting, gathering*
2) *assembly*
3) *collection*

собра́ть *see* собира́ть

собра́ться *see* собира́ться

^C со́бственно
1) *proper*
2) *strictly, properly*

со́бственно говоря́ = *as a matter of fact*

^A со́бственный *own*

^A собы́тие *event*

^C сова́ть (сую́, суёт, сую́т) / су́нуть (су́ну, су́нет, су́нут) *poke, thrust, slip*

^C соверша́ть / соверши́ть (совершу́, соверши́т, соверша́т)
1) *accomplish, perform, commit, make*
2) *strike (a bargain)*

^A соверше́нно *absolutely, quite, utterly, perfectly*

соверши́ть *see* соверша́ть

^B со́весть *(f.) conscience*

^A сове́т
1) *council*
2) *soviet, workers' council*

^B сове́товать (сове́тую, сове́тует, сове́туют), по- (кому́ / чему́) *advise (smb. / smth.)*

^A сове́тский
1) *Soviet Russian*
2) *Soviet*

совра́ть *see* **врать**

^B **совреме́нный** (совреме́нен, совреме́нна)
    1) *contemporary*
    2) *modern, up-to-date*

^A **совсе́м**
    1) *quite, entirely*
    2) совсе́м не *not at all, not a bit, not in the least*

^C **совхо́з** *(abbreviation of* сове́тское хозя́йство*)*
    state farm (in the USSR)

согласи́ться *see* **соглаша́ться**

^B **согла́сный** (согла́сен, согла́сна)
    быть согла́сным (с кем / чем) *agree (with smb./smth.)*

^A **соглаша́ться / согласи́ться** (соглашу́сь, согла-си́тся, согласи́тся, соглася́тся)
    1) (с кем / чем) *agree (with smb. | smth.)*
    2) (на что) *consent (to smth.)*

согре́ть *see* **греть**

^C **содержа́ние**
    1) *content, contents*
    2) *pay, salary, wages*

соедини́ть *see* **соединя́ть**

^B **соединя́ть / соедини́ть** (соединю́, соедини́т, сое-диня́т)
    1) *join, unite*
    2) *connect*
    3) *combine (chemistry)*

^A **сожале́ние**
    1) *regret*
    2) *pity*
    к сожале́нию = *unfortunately*

^A **создава́ть** (создаю́, создаёт, создаю́т; создава́й) / **созда́ть** (созда́м, созда́шь, созда́ст, созда-ди́м, создади́те, создаду́т; созда́й; со́здал, создала́, со́здало, со́здали) *create*

созда́ть *see* **создава́ть**

^B **созна́ние**
    1) *consciousness*

2) *confession*

сойти *see* **сходить**

^A **солдат** *(gen. pl.* солдат*) soldier*

^B **солнечный**

    1) *sun, solar*

    2) *sunny*

^A **солнце** *sun*

^B **соль** *(gen. pl.* солей*) salt*

    в чём здесь соль? = *what is the point?*

^C **сомневаться** *(ipf.)*

    (в ком / чём) *have doubts (as to smb. / smth.)*

^B **сомнение** *doubt*

^A **сон** *(gen.* сна*)*

    1) *sleep, slumber*

    2) *dream*

    видеть что-нибудь во сне = *dream something*

    видеть сон = *dream*

^A **сообщать / сообщить** (сообщу, сообщит, сообщат) *report, let know, inform*

^B **сообщение**

    1) *report, information*

    2) *communication*

сообщить *see* **сообщать**

сорвать *see* **срывать**

^B **соревнование** *competition, contest*

^A **сорок** *(gen.* сорока*) forty*

^A **сосед** *(pl. nom.* соседи, *gen.* соседей, *dat.* соседям*) neighbour*

^B **соседка** *(gen. pl.* соседок*) neighbour (ab. woman)*

^B **соседний** *neighbouring, adjacent*

^B **сосна** *(pl. nom.* сосны, *gen.* сосен*) pine-tree*

^C **состав**

    1) *composition, structure*

    2) *staff*

    3) *train*

составить *see* **составлять**

^A **составлять / составить** (составлю, составит, составят)

1) *put together, make up*

2) *constitute, form, be*

^в **состоя́ние**

    1) *state, condition*

    2) *fortune*

    он не в состоя́нии чита́ть = *he is not able to read*

^в **состоя́ть** *(only in the 3rd pers.:* состои́т, состоя́т*) (ipf.)*

    1) *(*из кого́ / чего́*) consist (of smb. / smth.)*

    2) *(*в чём*) consist (in smth.)*

^в **состоя́ться** *(only in the 3rd pers.:* состои́тся, состоя́тся*) (pf.) take place*

    сосчита́ть *see* **счита́ть**

^в **со́тня** *(gen. pl.* со́тен*) a hundred*

    сохрани́ть *see* **сохраня́ть**

^в **сохраня́ть / сохрани́ть** *(*сохраню́, сохрани́т, сохраня́т*) keep, preserve*

^в **социалисти́ческий** *socialist*

^с **сочине́ние** *(literary) work, writing, composition*

^в **сою́з**

    1) *union*

    2) *alliance*

^в **спаса́ть / спасти́** *(*спасу́, спасёт, спасу́т; спас, спасла́, спасло́, спасли́*) save, rescue*

^А **спаси́бо**

    1) *thank you*

    2) *thanks*

    спасти́ *see* **спаса́ть**

^А **спать** *(*сплю, спит, спят; спал, спала́, спа́ло, спа́ли*) sleep*

    он спал как уби́тый = *he was dead asleep*

^с **спекта́кль** *(m.) play, performance*

    спеть *see* **петь**

^с **специали́ст** *specialist, expert*

^в **специа́льность** *(f.)*

    1) *speciality*

    2) *profession, trade*

^В **специа́льный**
1) *special*
2) *professional*

^А **спеши́ть** (спешу́, спеши́т, спеша́т), **по-**
1) *hurry*
2) *be fast (ab. clock)*
де́лать что́-нибудь не спеша́ = *do smth. leisurely, do smth. without hurrying*

^А **спина́** *(sg. acc.* спи́ну, *gen.* спины́, *nom. pl.* спи́ны) *back*
узна́ть по со́бственной спине́ = *know from (bitter) experience*

^С **спи́чка** *(gen. pl.* спи́чек) *match*

^А **споко́йный** (споко́ен, споко́йна) *quiet, calm, tranquil*
споко́йной но́чи! = *good night!*

^В **спор** *(gen.* спо́ра / спо́ру) *argument*

^А **спо́рить** (спо́рю, спо́рит, спо́рят), **по-**
1) *argue, dispute*
2) *bet*

^А **спорт** *sport*

^А **спортсме́н** *sportsman*

^В **спо́соб** *way, method*

^А **спосо́бный** (спосо́бен, спосо́бна)
1) *clever, able*
2) (на что) *capable (of smth.)*

споткну́ться *see* **спотыка́ться**

^С **спотыка́ться** / **споткну́ться** (споткну́сь, споткнётся, споткну́тся) *stumble*

^А **спра́ва** *to the right*

^В **справедли́вый**
1) *just*
2) *correct*

спра́виться *see* **справля́ться**

^В **справля́ться** / **спра́виться** (спра́влюсь, спра́вится, спра́вятся)
1) (с чем) *cope (with smth.)*
2) (в чём) *look up (a word, etc.) (in smth.)*

^A **спра́шивать / спроси́ть** (спрошу́, спро́сит, спро́сят) *ask, inquire*

спроси́ть сове́та = *ask for advice*

спроси́ть *see* **спра́шивать**

спря́тать *see* **пря́тать**

^B **спуска́ться / спусти́ться** (спущу́сь, спу́стится, спу́стятся) *go down, descend*

спусти́ться *see* **спуска́ться**

^B **спустя́** *(prep. + acc.) after*

^C **спу́тник**

    1) *companion, fellow-traveller*

    2) *satellite*

^C **сра́внивать / сравни́ть** (сравню́, сравни́т, сравня́т)

    (кого́ / что с кем / чем)

    1) *compare (smb. | smth. with smb. | smth.)*

    2) *compare (smb. | smth. to smb. | smth.)*

сравни́ть *see* **сра́внивать**

^A **сра́зу** *at once*

^A **среда́** *(sg. acc.* сре́ду, *gen.* среды́, *pl. nom.* сре́ды, *dat.* среда́м) *Wednesday*

^A **среди́** *(prep. + gen.)*

    1) *in the middle of*

    2) *among*

^A **сре́дний**

    1) *middle, medium*

    2) *average*

^B **сре́дство**

    1) *means*

    2) *remedy*

    жить не по сре́дствам = *live beyond one's means*

    пуска́ть в ход все сре́дства = *leave no stone unturned*

^B **срок** *(gen.* сро́ка / сро́ку) *date, term, time*

^B **срыва́ть / сорва́ть** (сорву́, сорвёт, сорву́т)

1) *tear away, tear off, pick*
2) (что с кого) *cajole (smth. out of smb.)*
3) (что на ком / чём) *vent (one's anger, spleen, etc.) (upon smb. | smth.)*
4) *ruin*

^C **ссо́риться** (ссо́рюсь, ссо́рится, ссо́рятся), по- *quarrel*

^C **СССР** *(abbreviation of:* Сою́з Сове́тских Социалисти́ческих Респу́блик*)*
USSR (abbreviation of: Union of Soviet Socialist Republics)

^A **ста́вить** (ста́влю, ста́вит, ста́вят), по-
1) *put, place*
2) *set*
3) *produce*
4) *stake*
5) *raise*

^B **стадио́н** *stadium*

^A **стака́н** *glass, tumbler*

^A **станови́ться** (становлю́сь, стано́вится, стано́вятся) / **стать** (ста́ну, ста́нет, ста́нут)
1) *(only pf.) stop*
2) (кем / чем) *become (smb. | smth.)*
3) *(only pf.) begin*
4) *take one's stand*
5) *(only pf. and only impers.)* (с кем) *become of (smb.)*

ей ста́ло гру́стно = *she became sad*
ста́ло быть = *therefore, thus, consequently*

^A **ста́нция** *station*

^A **стара́ться,** по- *endeavour*

^A **стари́к** *(E) old man*

^C **стари́нный**
1) *ancient*
2) *antique*

^C **ста́роста**
1) *(in Pre-revolutionary Russia) village elder*

2) *monitor*

^B **стару́ха** *old woman*

ста́рше *see* **ста́рый**

^A **ста́рший**

    1) *oldest, eldest, elder, senior*

    2) *(used substantively, only pl.) elders*

^A **ста́рый** (стар, стара́, ста́ро, ста́ры; ста́рше) *old*

стать *see* **станови́ться**

^B **статья́** *(gen. pl.* статей*)*

    1) *article*

    2) *item*

    3) *clause*

^C **ствол**

    1) *trunk, stem*

    2) *barrel, gun tube*

^A **стекло́** *(pl. nom.* стёкла, *gen.* стёкол*)*

    1) *glass*

    2) *window-pane*

стемне́ть *see* **темне́ть**

^A **стена́** *(sg. acc.* сте́ну, *gen.* стены́, *pl. nom.* сте́ны, *dat.* стена́м*) wall*

^C **сте́пень** *(f.) (gen. pl.* степене́й*)*

    1) *degree*

    2) *power (mathematics)*

^B **степь** *(f.)* (в степи́; *gen. pl.* степе́й*) steppe*

стере́ть *see* **стира́ть**

^C **стира́ть / стере́ть** (сотру́, сотрёт, сотру́т; стёр, стёрла, стёрло, стёрли) *or* **вы́стирать**

    1) *(pf.* стере́ть*) wipe off, erase*

    2) *(pf.* вы́стирать*) wash*

^A **стих** *(E) verse*

^A **сто** *(gen.* ста*) a hundred*

^A **сто́ить** *(only in the 3rd pers.:* сто́ит, сто́ят*) (ipf.)*

    1) *(*что *or* чего́*) cost (smth.)*

    2) *(*чего́*) (only impers.) be worth (smth.)*

^A **стол** *(E) table*

^C **сто́лик** *small table*

^B **столи́ца** *capital*

^A **столóвая** *(adj. used substantively)*
  1) *dining-room*
  2) *dining-hall, canteen*

^A **стóлько** *so much, so many*

^C **стонáть** (стону́, стóнет, стóнут *or* стонáю, стонáет, стонáют) *(ipf.) moan, groan*

^A **сторонá** *(sg. acc.* стóрону, *gen.* стороны́, *pl. nom.* стóроны, *gen.* сторóн, *dat.* сторонáм) *side*

^A **стоя́ть** (стою́, стои́т, стоя́т) *(ipf.)*
  1) *stand*
  2) *lie*
  3) *be*
  4) *be at a standstill*
  стои́т прекрáсная погóда = *the weather is fine*

^B **страдáть, по-** *suffer*

^A **странá** *(pl.* стрáны) *country*
  стрáны свéта = *the four cardinal points*

^B **страни́ца** *page*

^A **стрáнный** (стрáнен, страннá, стрáнно) *strange*

^C **стрáстный** (стрáстен, страстнá, стрáстно) *passionate*

^B **страх** *fear, fright*
  под стрáхом смéрти = *on pain of death*

^A **стрáшный** (стрáшен, страшнá, стрáшно) *terrible, dreadful*
  мне стрáшно = *I am afraid*

  стрельну́ть *see* **стреля́ть**

^B **стреля́ть / стрельну́ть** (стрельну́, стрельнёт, стрельну́т) *shoot, fire*

^A **стреми́ться** (стремлю́сь, стреми́тся, стремя́тся) *(ipf.)*
  (к чему́) *aim (at smth.), aspire (to smth.), crave (for smth.)*

^C **стремлéние** *aspiration, striving*

^A **стрóгий** (строг, строгá, стрóго; стрóже) *strict, severe*

  стрóже *see* **стрóгий**

^B **строи́тель** *(m.) builder*

^в **строи́тельство**
   1) *building*
   2) *construction, project*

^А **стро́ить** (стро́ю, стро́ит, стро́ят), **вы́-, по-**
   build, construct

^С **строй** *system, order*

^В **стро́йка** *(gen. pl.* стро́ек*) (site for) building*

^С **стро́йный** (стро́ен, стройна́, стро́йно)
   1) *slender, well-proportioned*
   2) *well-composed*
   3) *harmonious*

^А **студе́нт** *student*

^В **стук** *knock, tap*

  сту́кнуть *see* **стуча́ть**

^А **стул** *(pl. nom.* сту́лья, *gen.* сту́льев*) chair*

^А **стуча́ть** (стучу́, стучи́т, стуча́т) / **сту́кнуть** (сту́кну, сту́кнет, сту́кнут) *knock*

^А **сты́дно** *(with the subject in dat.) feel ashamed*

^А **суббо́та** *Saturday*

^В **суд** *(Е)*
   1) *law-court*
   2) *trial*

^В **суди́ть** (сужу́, су́дит, су́дят) *(ipf.)*
   1) (о ком / чём) *estimate (smb. / smth.)*
   2) *judge*
   3) *referee*

^А **судьба́** *(pl. nom.* су́дьбы, *gen.* су́деб*) fate, fortune, destiny*

^В **судья́** *(pl. nom.* су́дьи, *gen.* суде́й, *dat.* су́дьям*)*
   1) *judge*
   2) *referee, umpire*

^В **суме́ть** (суме́ю, суме́ет, суме́ют) *(pf.) be able*

^В **су́мка** *(gen. pl.* су́мок*) bag*

  су́нуть *see* **сова́ть**

^С **суп** *(gen.* су́па / су́пу; в су́пе / в супу́; *pl. Е) soup*

^В **суро́вый**
   1) *severe, stern*
   2) *unbleached*

^B **су́тки** *(only pl.)* *(gen.* су́ток*)* *24 hours*

^A **сухо́й** (сух, суха́, су́хо; су́ше)
    1) *dry, arid*
    2) *reserved*

  су́ше *see* **сухо́й**

^B **существо́**
    1) *being, creature*
    2) *essence*

^B **существова́ть** (существу́ю, существу́ет, существу́ют) *(ipf.)* *exist, be*

  схвати́ть *see* **хвата́ть**

^B **сходи́ть** (схожу́, схо́дит, схо́дят) / **сойти́** (сойду́, сойдёт, сойду́т; сошёл, сошла́, сошло́, сошли́)
    1) (с чего́) *go, come, down (from smth.), get (off smth.)*
    2) (с чего́) *leave (smth.)*
    3) *(only in the 3rd pers.)* (на что) *descend (on smth.)*

    сойти́ с ума́ = *go mad*

^A **сце́на**
    1) *stage*
    2) *scene*

^A **счастли́вый** (сча́стлив, сча́стлива, сча́стливо, сча́стливы)
    1) *happy*
    2) *fortunate*

^A **сча́стье**
    1) *happiness*
    2) *luck, good fortune*

  счесть *see* **счита́ть**

  счёсться *see* **счита́ться**

^B **счёт** *(gen.* счёта / счёту; на счёте / на счету́; *pl.* счета́ / счёты*)*
    1) *(pl.* счета́*) calculation*
    2) *(pl.* счета́*) account*
    3) *(pl.* счета́*) score*
    4) *(only pl. and only* счёты*) abacus*

на свой счёт = *at one's own expense*

^A **счита́ть** / **счесть** (сочту́, сочтёт, сочту́т) *and*
сосчита́ть
1) *count*
2) (кого́ / что кем / чем) *consider (smb. / smth. smb. / smth.)*

^B **счита́ться, по-** *and* **счёсться** (сочту́сь, сочтётся, сочту́тся; счёлся, сочла́сь, сочло́сь, сочли́сь)
1) *(pf.* счёсться*)* (с кем / чем) *settle (accounts) (with smb. / smth.)*
2) *(pf.* по-*)* (с кем / чем) *take (smb. / smth.) into consideration*
3) *(only ipf.)* (кем / чем) *be considered (smb. / smth.)*

сшить *see* **шить**

^C **съезд** *congress, conference*

съесть *see* **есть**

сыгра́ть *see* **игра́ть**

^A **сын** *(pl. nom.* сыновья́*, gen.* сынове́й*) son*

^C **сыро́й** (сыр, сыра́, сы́ро)
1) *damp*
2) *raw, uncooked*
3) *raw (ab. material)*

^C **сы́тый** (сыт, сыта́, сы́то) *satisfied, replete*

^A **сюда́** *here*

Т

та *see* **тот**

^C **таба́к** *(gen.* табака́ / табаку́*) (E) tobacco*

^C **таи́нственный**
1) *mysterious, enigmatic*
2) *secret*

^A **та́йна** *secret, mystery*

^A **так**
1) *so, thus, like this*
2) *(followed by* как*) as*
так и быть = *all right, very well*
та́к-то и та́к-то = *in such and such a way*

так то́чно! = *yes, sir!*

^A та́кже *also, as well, too*

^A тако́й
1) *such*
2) *so*
что тако́е телеви́зор? = *what is a television set?*

^B такси́ *(indeclinable n.) taxi*

^B тала́нт *talent, gift*

^A там *there*

^B та́нец *(gen. та́нца) dance*

^A танцева́ть (танцу́ю, танцу́ет, танцу́ют) *(ipf.) dance*

^C таре́лка *(gen. pl. таре́лок) plate*

^A тащи́ть (тащу́, та́щит, та́щат), вы-
1) *drag*
2) *pull*

^C та́ять (та́ю, та́ет, та́ют), рас-
1) *(only in the 3rd pers.) melt*
2) *(only in the 3rd pers.) melt away, dwindle*
3) *(от чего́) melt (with smth.)*
4) *waste away*

^A твёрдый (твёрд, тверда́, твёрдо; твёрже) *hard, solid, firm*

твёрже *see* твёрдый

^A твой *(gen. твоего́; f. твоя́, gen. твое́й; n. твоё, gen. твоего́; pl. твои́, gen. твои́х) your, yours*

^B тво́рчество *creation, creative work, work*

те *see* тот

^B т.е. = то есть *that is (to say)*

^A теа́тр *theatre*

тебе́ *see* ты

тебя́ *see* ты

^A телеви́зор *television set*

^C теле́га *cart, waggon*

^C телегра́мма *telegram, wire*

^A телефо́н *telephone*

^B те́ло *(pl. тела́) body*

^A **тёма** subject, theme
^C **темнёть** (only in the 3rd pers.: темнёет, темнёют),
   по-, с-
   1) grow dark
   2) (only ipf.) appear dark, stand out dark
^A **темнота́** dark, darkness
^A **тёмный** (тёмен, темна́, тёмно́, тёмны́) dark
   тёмные лю́ди = ignorant people, people who
      can neither read nor write
   темны́м-темно́ = pitch-dark
^C **температу́ра** temperature
^B **тень** (f.) (в тени́; gen. pl. тене́й)
   1) shade
   2) shadow
^A **тепёрь** now, at present
^A **тёплый** (тёпел, тепла́, тёпло́, тёплы́)
   1) warm
   2) cordial
   мне тепло́ = I am warm
^B **терпели́вый** patient
^B **терпёть** (терплю́, тёрпит, тёрпят), **по-**
   1) suffer, endure
   2) stand
   3) tolerate
^A **теря́ть, по-** lose
^C **тёсный** (тёсен, тесна́, тёсно, тёсны́)
   1) narrow, tight
   2) (only the predicative forms) (too) narrow,
      (too) tight
^B **тетра́дь** (f.)
   1) writing-book, note-book, copy-book
   2) part
^A **тётя** (gen. pl. тётей) aunt
   тех see **тот**
^B **тёхника**
   1) technique
   2) technology
^B **тёхникум** technical schoo

^B тече́ние
1) *current*
2) *flow, course*
3) *trend, tendency*

^C течь *(only in the 3rd pers.:* течёт, теку́т; тёк, текла́, текло́, текли́*) (ipf.)*
1) *flow, run*
2) *leak*
3) *pass (ab. time)*

^C тип
1) *type*
2) *specimen*

^A ти́хий (тих, тиха́, ти́хо; ти́ше) *quiet, silent, soft, gentle, faint*

ти́ше *see* ти́хий

^A тишина́ *silence*

^C ткань *(f.) cloth, fabric, material*

то *see* тот

^A то *then, or not translated*
то ... то = *now ... now, sometimes ... sometimes*
то и де́ло = *incessantly, perpetually*
а то = *otherwise*
-то = *just, precisely*

тобо́й *see* ты

тобо́ю *see* ты

^C това́р *goods*

^A това́рищ *comrade, friend*

^A тогда́ *then, at that time*
тогда́ как = *though*

того́ *see* тот

^A то́же *also, too, as well*

той *see* тот

^A толка́ть / толкну́ть (толкну́, толкнёт, толкну́т)
1) *push, shove*
2) *incite, instigate*

толкну́ть *see* толка́ть

^A толпа́ *(pl.* то́лпы*) crowd*

^A **то́лстый** (толст, толста́, то́лсто, то́лсты; то́лще)
   thick, stout

то́лще *see* **то́лстый**

^A **то́лько** *only*
   и заче́м то́лько она́ так сказа́ла? = *why on
      earth did she say so?*
   то́лько что = *just, just now*
   как то́лько = *as soon as*
   они́ уе́хали то́лько вчера́ = *they left only
      yesterday*

^B **тон** *(pl.* то́ны / тона́) *tone*

^A **то́нкий** (то́нок, тонка́, то́нко; то́ньше)
   1) *thin*
   2) *slender*
   3) *delicate*
   4) *subtle*

^C **тону́ть** (тону́, то́нет, то́нут), **по-, у-**
   1) *sink (to the bottom)*
   2) *get drowned*

то́ньше *see* **то́нкий**

^C **то́поль** *(m.) (pl.* тополя́) *poplar*

^C **торго́вля** *trade, commerce*

^A **торже́ственный**
   1) *festive*
   2) *solemn*

^B **торопи́ться** (тороплю́сь, торо́пится, торо́пятся),
   по- *hurry, hasten*

^B **торопли́вый** *hasty, hurried*

^B **торча́ть** (торчу́, торчи́т, торча́т) *(ipf.)* *jut out,
   protrude, stick out, be seen*

^B **тоска́** *melancholy, yearning*

^A **тот** *(gen.* того́; *f.* та, *gen.* той; *n.* то, *gen.* того́;
   pl. те, *gen.* тех) *that*
   я говорю́ о том, что... = *I am speaking about
      the fact that...*
   тот же = тот же са́мый = *the same*
   де́ло в том, что... = *the fact is that...*

мне не до того́ = *I have other things to attend to*

и тому́ подо́бное (и т. п.) = *and so on*

вме́сто того́, что́бы... = *instead of...*

тем не ме́нее = *nevertheless*

по́сле того́ как... = *after...*

до того́ как... = пе́ред тем как... = *before...*

в то вре́мя как... = *while...*

^В то́тчас *at once*

^В то́чка *(gen. pl.* то́чек*) point, full stop*

^А то́чно
1) *exactly, precisely*
2) *as though, as if*

^В то́чный (то́чен, точна́, то́чно) *exact, precise*
то́чные нау́ки = *the exact sciences*

^А трава́ *(pl.* тра́вы*)*
1) *grass*
2) *(only pl.) herbs*

^С трактори́ст *tractor driver*

^В трамва́й *tram*

^С тра́тить (тра́чу, тра́тит, тра́тят), **ис-** *spend*

^А тре́бовать (тре́бую, тре́бует, тре́буют), **по-** (чего́) *demand (smth.)*

^В трево́га *alarm, anxiety, uneasiness*

^А трево́жный (трево́жен, трево́жна)
1) *anxious*
2) *alarming*
3) *(only the attributive forms) alarm*

трём *see* **три**

трёмста́м *see* **три́ста**

тремя́ *see* **три**

тремяста́ми *see* **три́ста**

^А тре́тий *(f.* тре́тья, *n.* тре́тье*) third*
в-тре́тьих = *in the third place, thirdly*

трёх *see* **три**

трёхсо́т *see* **три́ста**

трёхста́х *see* **три́ста**

^А три *(gen., the prepositional case* трёх, *dat.* трём,

instr. тремя́) *three*

^A **три́дцать** *(gen.* тридцати́*) thirty*

^B **три́ста** *(gen.* трёхсо́т, *dat.* трёмста́м, *instr.* тремяста́ми, *the prepositional case* трёхста́х*) three hundred*

^C **тро́гать / тро́нуть** (тро́ну, тро́нет, тро́нут) *touch, move*

^B **тро́е** *(gen., the prepositional case* трои́х, *dat.* трои́м, *instr.* трои́ми*) three*

　трои́м *see* **тро́е**

　трои́ми *see* **тро́е**

　трои́х *see* **тро́е**

^A **тролле́йбус** *trolleybus*

　тро́нуть *see* **тро́гать**

^C **тротуа́р** *pavement*

^B **труба́** *(pl.* тру́бы*)*
　　1) *pipe, tube, chimney, funnel*
　　2) *trumpet*

^B **тру́бка** *(gen. pl.* тру́бок*)*
　　1) *small tube*
　　2) *(tobacco) pipe*
　　3) *(telephone) receiver*
　　4) *trumpet*

^A **труд** *(E)*
　　1) *labour, work*
　　2) *trouble*
　　3) *(scientific) work*

^C **труди́ться** (тружу́сь, тру́дится, тру́дятся) *(ipf.)* *work, labour*

^A **тру́дный** (тру́ден, трудна́, тру́дно, тру́дны) *difficult, hard*

^C **трудово́й**
　　1) *working*
　　2) *labour*

^C **трясти́** (трясу́, трясёт, трясу́т; тряс, трясла́, трясло́, трясли́), **вы-** *and* **тряхну́ть** (тряхну́, тряхнёт, тряхну́т)
　　1) *(pf.* тряхну́ть*) shake*

2) *(pf.* вы́-*)* (что из чего́) *shake (smth. out of smth.)*

тряхну́ть *see* **трясти́**

^A **туда́** *there, that way*

^A **тума́н** *mist, fog, haze*

^C **тупо́й** (туп, тупа́, ту́по)
  1) *blunt*
  2) *obtuse*
  3) *dull, stupid, slow-witted*
  4) *dull (ab. pain)*

^C **тури́ст** *tourist*

^A **тут** *here*
  тут же = *there and then*
  и всё тут = *there is nothing to be done*

^C **ту́фля** *(gen. pl.* ту́фель*) (lady's) shoe*

^C **ту́ча** *(black) cloud, storm-cloud*

^C **тща́тельный** (тща́телен, тща́тельна) *careful, painstaking*

^A **ты** *(acc., gen.* тебя́*, dat., the prepositional case* тебе́*, instr.* тобо́й / тобо́ю*) you*

^A **ты́сяча** *(instr.* ты́сячей / ты́сячью*) a thousand*

^C **тюрьма́** *(pl. nom.* тю́рьмы*, gen.* тю́рем*) prison*

^A **тяжёлый** (тяжёл, тяжела́)
  1) *heavy*
  2) *hard, difficult*

^C **тя́жесть** *(f.)*
  1) *weight, heaviness*
  2) *gravity*
  3) *(mostly used in the pl.) heavy object*

^A **тяну́ть** (тяну́, тя́нет, тя́нут) *(ipf.)*
  1) *pull*
  2) *draw*
  3) *drawl, drag out*
  4) *(impers.)* (чем) тя́нет хо́лодом от о́кон *there is a cold draught from the windows*

^B **тяну́ться, по-** (тяну́сь, тя́нется, тя́нутся)
  1) *stretch*

2) (к кому́ / чему́)   *reach (for smb. | smth.),*
strive (after smb. | smth.)

У

^A **у** *(prep. + gen.) by, with*
у него́ мно́го де́нег = *he has much money*
стоя́ть у две́ри = *stand in the doorway*

^A **убега́ть / убежа́ть** (убегу́, убежи́т, убегу́т) *run
away, escape*

убеди́ть *see* **убежда́ть**

убежа́ть *see* **убега́ть**

^B **убежда́ть / убеди́ть** *(not used in the 1st pers. sg.,*
убеди́т, убедя́т*)*
1) *convince*
2) *persuade*

^A **убива́ть / уби́ть** (убью́, убьёт, убью́т; убе́й)
1) *kill*
2) *make, broken-hearted*
3) *waste, squander*

^B **убира́ть / убра́ть** (уберу́, уберёт, уберу́т; убра́л,
убрала́, убра́ло, убра́ли)
1) *take away, remove*
2) *gather in, harvest*
3) *tidy up*
4) *decorate*
убра́ть посте́ль = *make the bed*

уби́ть *see* **убива́ть**

убра́ть *see* **убира́ть**

^B **уважа́ть** *(ipf.) respect, esteem*

^A **уве́ренный** *assured, sure, confident, certain*

уве́рить *see* **уверя́ть**

^B **уверя́ть / уве́рить** (уве́рю, уве́рит, уве́рят) *assure,
make believe*

увида́ть *see* **вида́ть**

уви́деть *see* **ви́деть**

^C **увлека́ться / увле́чься** (увлеку́сь,   увлечётся,
увлеку́тся;   увлёкся,   увлекла́сь,   увлекло́сь,
увлекли́сь)

1) (кем / чем) *be keen on (smb. / smth.)*

2) (кем) *fall in love with (smb.)*

увлечься *see* **увлекаться**

^C **уговаривать / уговорить** (уговорю, уговорит, уговорят) *persuade*

уговорить *see* **уговаривать**

^A **угол** (в, на, углу; в угле; *E*)

1) (в, на, углу) *corner*

2) (в угле) *angle*

ходить из угла в угол = *walk up and down (in a state af anxiety)*

угостить *see* **угощать**

^B **угощать / угостить** (угощу, угостит, угостят) (кого / что чем) *treat (smb. / smth. to smth.)*

^C **угрюмый** *sullen, gloomy*

^A **удаваться** *(only in the 3rd pers.:* удаётся, удаются) / **удаться** *(only in the 3rd pers.:* удастся, удадутся; удался, удалась, удалось, удались)

1) *turn out well, be a success*

2) *(impers.,* кому / чему) ему удалось найти книгу *he succeeded in finding the book*

удалить *see* **удалять**

^C **удалять / удалить** (удалю, удалит, удалят)

1) *remove*

2) *make leave, send away*

^B **удар**

1) *blow*

2) *(apoplectic) stroke*

быть в ударе = *be in good form*

ударить *see* **ударять**

^A **ударять / ударить** (ударю, ударит, ударят) *strike, hit*

удаться *see* **удаваться**

удержать *see* **удерживать**

^C **удерживать / удержать** (удержу, удержит, удержат)

1) *retain, hold*

2) *suppress*

3) *keep*

^A удиви́тельный (удиви́телен, удиви́тельна)
astonishing, surprising

удиви́ться *see* удивля́ться

^A удивле́ние *astonishment, surprise*

^B удивлённый *surprised*

^A удивля́ться / удиви́ться (удивлю́сь, удиви́тся,
удивя́тся)
(кому́ / чему́) *be astonished (at smb. | smth.)*

^B удо́бный (удо́бен, удо́бна)
1) *comfortable*
2) *convenient*

^A удово́льствие *pleasure*

^C уе́зд *district*

^A уезжа́ть / уе́хать (уе́ду, уе́дет, уе́дут; уезжа́й)
leave, go away

уж *see* уже́

^A у́жас *terror, horror*

у́же *see* у́зкий

^A уже́ (уж)
1) *already, by now*
2) *really*
уже́ не = *no longer*

^C у́жин *supper*

^A у́зкий (у́зок, узка́, у́зко́, у́зки; у́же)
1) *narrow, tight*
2) *(only* у́зок *and the predicative forms with
stressed endings) too narrow, too tight*

^A узнава́ть (узнаю́, узнаёт, узнаю́т; узнава́й)
/ узна́ть
1) *recognize*
2) *learn, know*

узна́ть *see* узнава́ть

уйти́ *see* уходи́ть

указа́ть *see* ука́зывать

^A ука́зывать / указа́ть (укажу́, ука́жет, ука́жут)
1) (на кого́ / что) *point (at, to, smb. | smth.)*
2) *indicate, point out, explain*

170

^C укла́дывать / уложи́ть (уложу́, уло́жит, уло́жат)
  1) *lay*
  2) (что) *put (smth.) where it belongs*
  3) *pack up*
  4) (чем) *cover (with smth.)*

укра́сть *see* кра́сть

^A у́лица *street*

уложи́ть *see* укла́дывать

^A улыба́ться / улыбну́ться (улыбну́сь, улыбнётся, улыбну́тся) *smile*

^A улы́бка *(gen. plur.* улы́бок) *smile*

улыбну́ться *see* улыба́ться

^B ум *(E) wit, intellect*

^C уменьша́ть / уме́ньшить (уме́ньшу, уме́ньшит, уме́ньшат) *diminish, reduce*

уме́ньшить *see* уменьша́ть

умере́ть *see* умира́ть

^A уме́ть (уме́ю, уме́ет, уме́ют) *(ipf.) be able (to do smth. one has learnt to do), know*

^A умира́ть / умере́ть (умру́, умрёт, умру́т; у́мер, умерла́, у́мерло, у́мерли) *die*

^A у́мный (умён, умна́, у́мно́, у́мны́) *clever*

^C умыва́ться / умы́ться (умо́юсь, умо́ется, умо́ются) *wash oneself*

умы́ться *see* умыва́ться

^B университе́т *university*

упа́сть *see* па́дать

уплати́ть *see* плати́ть

употреби́ть *see* употребля́ть

^C употребля́ть / употреби́ть (употреблю́, употреби́т, употребя́т) *use*

^C управле́ние *management, government, direction*

^C упря́мый *obstinate, stubborn*

^C у́ровень *(gen.* у́ровня)
  1) *level*
  2) *standard*

^C урожа́й *harvest*

^A уро́к

1) *lesson*
2) *home work, task*
вот тебе́ уро́к = *let that be a lesson to you*
урони́ть *see* **рони́ть**
ᶜ **уса́дьба** *(gen. pl.* **уса́деб***)*
   1) *farmstead*
   2) *(old) country seat*
   3) *main building, dwelling house (of farmstead or country seat)*
ᴮ **уси́лие** *effort*
ᴬ **усло́вие** *condition*
   услы́шать *see* **слы́шать**
ᴮ **усмеха́ться / усмехну́ться** (усмехну́сь, усмехнёт-ся, усмехну́тся) *smile (ironically), grin*
   усмехну́ться *see* **усмеха́ться**
ᶜ **усну́ть** (усну́, уснёт, усну́т) *(pf.)*
   1) *fall asleep*
   2) *die (ab. fish)*
ᴬ **успева́ть / успе́ть** (успе́ю, успе́ет, успе́ют)
   1) *have time, be in time*
   2) *(only ipf.) make progress (at school, in a subject)*
   успе́ть *see* **успева́ть**
ᴬ **успе́х**
   1) *success, (good) luck*
   2) *(only pl.) progress*
ᴮ **успока́иваться / успоко́иться** (успоко́юсь, успо-ко́ится, успоко́ятся)
   1) *calm*
   2) *abate, calm down*
   3) *rest*
   успоко́иться *see* **успока́иваться**
ᴮ **устава́ть** (устаю́, устаёт, устаю́т; устава́й) / **уста́ть** (уста́ну, уста́нет, уста́нут) *get tired*
ᴬ **уста́лый** *tired*
ᴮ **устана́вливать / установи́ть** (установлю́, устано́-вит, устано́вят)
   1) *place, mount, install, set*

2) *establish*

3) *determine, fix, ascertain*

установи́ть *see* **устана́вливать**

уста́ть *see* **устава́ть**

^A **устра́ивать / устро́ить** (устро́ю, устро́ит, устро́ят)

    1) (что) *arrange (smth.)*

    2) (что) *make (smth.), cause (smth.)*

    3) (кого́) *place (smb.), fix (smb.) up*

    он устро́ил его́ на рабо́те = *he has found work for him*

устро́ить *see* **устра́ивать**

^C **усы́** *(m. pl.)*

    1) *moustache*

    2) *whiskers*

    3) *antennae*

    в ус (себе́) не дуть = *not care a straw*

^B **утеша́ть / уте́шить** (уте́шу, уте́шит, уте́шат) *comfort, console*

уте́шить *see* **утеша́ть**

утону́ть *see* **тону́ть**

^C **у́тренний** *morning*

^A **у́тро** (с утра́; до утра́; от утра́; к утру́; по утра́м) *morning*

    у́тром = *in the morning*

^C **уха́живать** *(ipf.)*

    (за кем / чем)

    1) *look after (smb. / smth.)*

    2) *court (smb. / smth.)*

^A **у́хо** *(nom. pl.* у́ши, *gen.* уше́й*) ear*

^A **уходи́ть** (ухожу́, ухо́дит, ухо́дят) **/ уйти́** (уйду́, уйдёт, уйду́т; ушёл, ушла́, ушло́, ушли́) *go away, leave*

    доро́га ухо́дит в лес = *the road leads into the wood*

^B **уча́ствовать** (уча́ствую, уча́ствует, уча́ствуют) *(ipf.)*

    (в чём) *take part (in smth.)*

^A **уча́стие** *participation, collaboration*

^B **уча́стник** *participant*

^B **уча́сток** *(gen.* уча́стка*)*
    1) *lot, plot, parcel*
    2) *part, section*
    3) *district*

^C **уча́щийся** *(present participle used substantively)*
    pupil, student

^C **уче́бник** *text-book, manual*

^C **уче́бный** *educational, school*

^A **учени́к** *(E) pupil*

^B **учени́ца** *pupil (ab. girl)*

^A **учёный**
    1) *learned, erudite, scientific*
    2) *(used substantively) scientist, scholar*

^A **учи́тель** *(pl.* учителя́*) teacher*

^A **учи́тельница** *teacher (ab. woman)*

^A **учи́ть** (учу́, у́чит, у́чат), **вы́-, на-, об-**
    1) *(pf.* вы́-, на-, об-*) (кого чему) teach (smb.*
    smth.)
    2) *(pf.* вы́-*) (что) learn (smth.)*

^A **учи́ться** (учу́сь, у́чится, у́чатся), **вы́-, на-, об-**
    1) *(чему́) learn (smth.)*
    2) *go to school*
    век живи́ - век учи́сь = *live and learn*

^C **ую́тный** (ую́тен, ую́тна) *comfortable, cosy*

Ф

^B **фа́брика** *factory, mill*

^B **факт** *fact*

^C **факульте́т** *faculty, department*

^A **фами́лия** *surname, family name*

^C **фаши́ст** *fascist*

^A **февра́ль** *(gen.* февраля́*) February*

^C **фе́рма**
    1) *farm*
    2) *special farm at a kolkhoz*

^в **фигу́ра** *figure*

^с **фи́зика** *physics*

^А **фильм** *film*

^с **флаг** *flag*

^с **флот** *(gen. pl.* флото́в*) fleet*

^с **фона́рь** *(gen.* фонаря́*) lantern, lamp*

^с **фонта́н** *fountain*

^А **фо́рма**
1) *form*
2) *mould*
3) *uniform*

^с **фо́рточка** *(gen. pl.* фо́рточек*) top light*

^с **фотоаппара́т** *camera*

^в **фотогра́фия** *photography*

^в **фра́за**
1) *sentence*
2) *phrase*

^А **францу́з** *Frenchman*

^в **фронт** *(gen. pl.* фронто́в*) front*

^в **фрукт** *fruit*

^А **футбо́л** *football*

X

^с **хала́т**
1) *dressing-gown*
2) *bath-robe*
3) *overalls*
4) *smock, (white) coat*

^А **хара́ктер**
1) *disposition, temper, character*
2) *nature*

^с **хвали́ть** (хвалю́, хва́лит, хва́лят), **по-** *praise, commend*

^А **хва́тать / схвати́ть** (схвачу́, схва́тит, схва́тят) *or* **хвати́ть** (хвачу́, хва́тит, хва́тят)
1) *(pf.* схвати́ть *or* хвати́ть*) snatch, seize*
2) *(pf.* хвати́ть, *and only used in the 3rd pers.)*

(кому́ чего́) *be sufficient (for smb.)*

ему́ хвати́ло вре́мени = *he had time enough*

и до́ма де́ла хва́тит = *there is plenty to do at home, too*

у *(or:* с*)* него́ не хвата́ет де́нег = *he is short of money*

хва́тит! = *that will do!*

с меня́ хва́тит! = *I have had enough!*

хвати́ть *see* хвата́ть

^B хвост *(E)*
  1) *tail*
  2) *line, queue*

^C хи́мия *chemistry*

^B хи́трый (хитёр, хитра́, хи́тро́, хи́тры́)
  1) *sly, cunning*
  2) *intricate*

^A хлеб
  1) *bread, loaf*
  2) *(pl.* хлеба́*) corn, grain*
  хлеб-со́ль = *hospitality*

^C хло́пать / хло́пнуть (хло́пну, хло́пнет, хло́пнут)
  1) (кого́ / что по чему́) *slap (smb. / smth. on smth.)*
  2) (чем) *bang (smth.)*

хло́пнуть *see* хло́пать

^C хму́риться (хму́рюсь, хму́рится, хму́рятся), на-
  1) *frown*
  2) *(only in the 3rd pers.) gloom, be overcast*

^A ход (на хо́де / ходу́)
  1) (на ходу́) *motion, working, run*
  2) (в, на, хо́де) *course*

^A ходи́ть (хожу́, хо́дит, хо́дят) *(indet. vb. of motion) (ipf.)*
  1) *go, walk*
  2) (в чём) *wear (smth.)*

^A хозя́ин *(pl. nom.* хозя́ева*, gen.* хозя́ев*, dat.* хозя́евам*)*
  1) *owner, proprietor, master*
  2) *host*

^B **хозя́йка** *(gen. pl. хозя́ек)*
1) *owner, proprietress, mistress*
2) *hostess*

^B **хозя́йство**
1) *economy*
2) *farm*
3) *household, (domestic) establishment*
4) *enterprise*

^C **хо́лод** *(pl. холода́)*
1) *(only sg.) cold, coldness*
2) *cold weather, cold air*

^A **холо́дный** (хо́лоден, холодна́, хо́лодно, хо́лодны) *cold*

^C **хор** *(pl. хо́ры)*
1) *chorus*
2) *choir*

^A **хоро́ший** (хоро́ш, хороша́; лу́чше) *good*
всего́ хоро́шего! = *(I wish you) all the best!*
good-bye!

^A **хоте́ть** (хочу́, хо́чешь, хо́чет, хоти́м, хоти́те, хотя́т) *(ipf.) want*

^A **хоте́ться** *(only in the 3rd pers. sg.:* хо́чется) *(ipf.)*
(impers., кому́ / чему́*)* мне хо́чется пойти́ в
теа́тр *I want to go to the theatre, I should like
to go to the theatre*

^A **хоть**
1) *though*
2) *at least*
хоть кто = *anybody*

^A **хотя́** *though*

^C **хра́брый** (храбр, храбра́, хра́бро) *brave, valiant*

^B **худо́жественный**
1) *artistic*
2) *(only the attributive forms) art*
худо́жественная литерату́ра = *fiction*

^A **худо́жник**
1) *artist*
2) *painter*

^в **худо́й** (худ, худа́, ху́до) *lean, thin, emaciated*
ху́же *see* **плохо́й**

Ц

^с **ца́рство**
    1) *empire (of the Tsar)*
    2) *realm, kingdom*

^в **царь** *(gen.* царя́*)*
    1) *tsar*
    2) *king*

^А **цвет** *(pl.* цвета́*) colour*
    како́го цве́та каранда́ш? = *what colour is the
    pencil*

^А **цвето́к** *(gen.* цветка́*, pl. nom.* цветы́*, gen.* цвето́в*)
    flower, blossom*

^в **целова́ть** (целу́ю, целу́ет, целу́ют), **по-** *kiss*

^А **це́лый** (цел, цела́, це́ло)
    1) *(only the attributive forms) whole, entire*
    2) *intact, safe*
    в о́бщем и це́лом = *in general*

^А **цель** *(f.)*
    1) *aim, object, end*
    2) *objective*
    3) *target*

^с **цена́** *(sg. acc.* це́ну*, gen.* цены́*, nom. pl.* це́ны*)*
    1) *price*
    2) *worth, value*

^в **центр** *centre*

^с **цепь** *(f.)* (в, на, цепи́; *gen. pl.* цепе́й) *chain,
    bonds, fetters*

^в **це́рковь** *(sg. gen., dat., the prepositional case*
    це́ркви, *instr.* це́рковью, *pl. nom.* це́ркви, *gen.*
    церкве́й, *dat.* церква́м*) church*

^с **цех** (в це́хе / цеху́; *pl.* це́хи / цеха́) *(work)shop,
    department (of factory)*

^с **цирк** *circus*

^с **ци́фра** *figure, cipher*

Ч

A **чай** *(gen.* чáя / чáю*)* *tea*

C **чáйник** *tea-pot, tea-kettle*

A **час** *(gen.* чáса / часý / *(after cardinal numbers)*
часá; в чáсе / часý; *pl. E) hour*
в час (дня) = *at one o'clock (in the afternoon)*
котóрый час? = *what time is it?*
в пятом часý = *between 4 and 5 o'clock*
часы́ пик = *the rush hours*
часы́ = *clock, watch*

A **чáстый** (част, частá, чáсто; чáще)
1) *frequent*
2) *close*
3) *quick, fast*

A **часть** *(gen. pl.* частéй*) part*

C **чáшка** *(gen. pl.* чáшек*)*
1) *cup*
2) *scale*

чáще *see* **чáстый**

чегó *see* **что**

B **чей** *(f.* чья, *n.* чьё, *pl.* чьи*) whose*

A **человéк** *(only used in the sg.;* люди *is used as
the pl.; the gen. pl. form* человéк *is, however,
used after cardinal numbers) person, man*

C **человéчество** *mankind, humanity*

чем *see* **что**

чём *see* **что**

A **чем** *than*
чем бóльше, тем лýчше = *the more the better*

B **чемодáн** *trunk, suitcase*

чемý *see* **что**

C **чепухá** *nonsense*

A **чéрез** *(prep.* + *acc.)*
1) *over, across*
2) *through*
3) *(indicating time) in*
4) *every other, every second (ab. time)*

перейти через площадь = *walk across the square*

ехать через город = *drive through the town*

я вернусь через час = *I'll be back in an hour*

ходить в школу через день = *go to school every second day*

A **чёрный** (чёрен, черна, чёрно, чёрны) *black*

чёрная работа = *unskilled labour*

чёрный ход = *back entrance, kitchen door*

B **чёрт** (*pl. nom.* черти, *gen.* чертей) *devil*

что за чёрт! = *hang it! damn!*

B **черта** *(E)*

1) *line*
2) *boundary, precinct*
3) *trait, feature*

A **честный** (честен, честна, честно) *honest*

B **честь** (*f.*) (в чести) *honour*

A **четверг** *(E) Thursday*

C **четверо** (*gen.* четверых) *four*

A **четвёртый** *fourth*

C **четверть** (*f.*) (*gen. pl.* четвертей) *fourth, quarter*

A **четыре** (*gen.*, *the prepositional case* четырёх, *dat.* четырём, *instr.* четырьмя) *four*

четырём *see* **четыре**

четырёмстам *see* **четыреста**

A **четыреста** (*gen.* четырёхсот, *dat.* четырёмстам, *instr.* четырьмястами, *the prepositional case* четырёхстах) *four hundred*

четырёх *see* **четыре**

четырёхсот *see* **четыреста**

четырёхстах *see* **четыреста**

B **четырнадцать** (*gen.* четырнадцати) *fourteen*

четырьмя *see* **четыре**

четырьмястами *see* **четыреста**

C **чиновник**

1) *official (in Pre-revolutionary Russia; in the USSR the word is only used about foreign officials)*

2) *bureaucrat*

^A **числó** *(pl. nom.* чи́сла, *gen.* чи́сел*)*
1) *number*
2) *date*
в том числé = *including*

^C **чи́стить** (чи́щу, чи́стит, чи́стят), **вы́-, о-, по-**
1) *(pf.* вы́-, по-*) clean, brush*
2) *(pf.* о-*) peel*

^C **чистотá**
1) *cleanness*
2) *cleanliness, neatness*
3) *purity*

^A **чи́стый** (чист, чистá, чи́сто, чи́сты; чи́ще)
1) *clean*
2) *pure*
3) *clear*

^B **читáтель** *(m.) reader*

^A **читáть, про-** *or* **прочéсть** (прочтý, прочтёт, прочтýт) *read*

  чи́ще *see* **чи́стый**

^C **член**
1) *member*
2) *extremity*

^C **чрезвычáйный** (чрезвычáен, чрезвычáйна) *extraordinary*

^C **чтéние**
1) *reading*
2) *reading (aloud)*
3) *(only pl.) lectures*

^A **что** *(gen.* чегó, *dat.* чемý, *instr.* чем, *the prepositional case* о чём*)*
1) *what*
2) *what, which, that*
ни за что = *by no means*

^A **что** *that*

  чтоб *see* **чтóбы**

^A **чтóбы** (чтоб)
1) *that*

2) *in order (to) or not translated*

^A **чтó-нибудь** *(as for the declination, see* что*) something, anything*

^A **чтó-то** *(as for the declination, see* что*) something*

^A **чýвство** *sense, feeling*

^A **чýвствовать** (чýвствую, чýвствует, чýвствуют) *(ipf.) feel*

    чудесá *see* **чýдо**

^B **чудéсный** (чудéсен, чудéсна) *wonderful*

^C **чýдо** *(pl. nom.* чудесá, *gen.* чудéс*) miracle, wonder*

^A **чужóй** *strange, somebody else's, another's*

^C **чулóк** *(gen. sg.* чулкá, *gen. pl.* чулóк*) stocking*

^A **чуть** *hardly, slightly, just*

    он чуть не упáл = *he nearly fell*

    чуть-чуть = *a little (bit), nearly*

Ш

^A **шаг** *(gen.* шáга / шáгу *(after cardinal numbers)* шагá; на, в, шагý) *(pl. E) step, pace*

    прибáвить шáгу = *quicken one's pace*

^B **шагáть / шагнýть** (шагнý, шагнёт, шагнýт)

    1) *(only ipf.) step, walk, stride*

    2) *(чéрез что) step (over, across, smth.)*

  шагнýть *see* **шагáть**

^A **шáпка** *(gen. pl.* шáпок*) cap*

^C **шар** *(pl. E)*

    1) *ball*

    2) *globe*

^C **шáхматы** *(only pl.) (gen.* шáхмат*) chess*

^C **шевелúть** (шевелю́, шевéлит, шевéлят) / **по-** *and* **шевельнýть** (шевельнý, шевельнёт, шевельнýт) *or* **пошевельнýть**

    1) *(pf.* пошевелúть*) turn, ted*

    2) *(pf.* шевельнýть *or* пошевельнýть*) (чем) move (smth.) (slightly), stir (smth.)*

  шевельнýть *see* **шевелúть**

^C **шёлковый** *silk*

  шепнýть *see* **шептáть**

^B **шёпотом** *in a whisper, under one's breath*

^B **шепта́ть** (шепчу́, ше́пчет, ше́пчут) / **шепну́ть** (шепну́, шепнёт, шепну́т) *whisper*

^A **шесто́й** *sixth*

^A **шесть** *(gen.* шести́*) six*

^B **ше́я** *(gen. pl.* шей*) neck*
    сиде́ть на ше́е у роди́телей = *hang on to one's parents*

  ши́ре *see* **широ́кий**

^A **широ́кий** (широ́к, широка́, широ́ко́, широ́ки́; ши́ре)
    1) *wide, broad*
    2) *great, on a large scale*
    3) *(only the predicative forms with stressed endings) too wide, too broad*

^C **шить** (шью, шьёт, шьют; шей), **с-** (сошью́, сошьёт, сошью́т; соше́й) *sew*

^B **шкаф** (в шкафу́; *pl. E) cupboard*

^A **шко́ла** *school*

^A **шко́льник** *schoolboy*

^B **шля́па** *hat*

^A **шокола́д** *chocolate*

^C **шоссе́** *(indeclinable n.) highway*

^A **шофёр** *chauffeur, driver*

^B **шту́ка**
    1) *piece*
    2) *thing*
    3) *"chap"*
    4) *(only pl.) trick*
    в то́м-то и шту́ка! = *that is just the point!*

^B **шу́ба** *fur coat*

^A **шум** *(gen.* шу́ма / шу́му*)*
    1) *noise*
    2) *uproar*

^B **шуме́ть** (шумлю́, шуми́т, шумя́т) *(ipf.) make noise*

^A **шути́ть, по-** (шучу́, шу́тит, шу́тят) *joke*
    говори́ть не шутя́ = *speak quite seriously*

^B шу́тка *(gen. pl.* шу́ток*) joke*
 кро́ме шу́ток = *joking apart*

Щ

^A щека́ *(sg. acc.* щёку*, gen.* щеки́*, pl. nom.* щёки*, dat.* щека́м*) cheek*

Э

^B экза́мен *examination, exam*
 вы́держать экза́мен = *pass an examition*
 сдать экза́мен = *sit for an examination*
^C экску́рсия *excursion, trip*
^C экспеди́ция
  1) *expedition*
  2) *dispatch office*
^C электри́ческий *electric, electrical*
^C электри́чка *(gen. pl.* электри́чек*)*
  1) *electric train*
  2) *underground, tube*
^B электроста́нция *electric power station*
^C эне́ргия *energy*
^C эпо́ха *epoch, age, era*
 э́та *see* э́тот
^B эта́ж *(E) floor, storey*
 второ́й эта́ж = *the first floor*
 э́ти *see* э́тот
 э́тих *see* э́тот
 э́то *see* э́тот
 э́того *see* э́тот
 э́той *see* э́тот
^A э́тот *(gen.* э́того*; f.* э́та*, gen.* э́той*; n.* э́то*, gen.* э́того*; pl.* э́ти*, gen.* э́тих*)*
  1) *this, that*
  2) *(only* э́то*) this (that, it) is*

Ю

^C ю́бка *(gen. pl.* ю́бок*) skirt*
^A юг *south*

184

^C **ю́жный** *southern, south*

^B **ю́ноша** *(gen. pl.* ю́ношей*) youth*

^A **ю́ный** (юн, юна́, ю́но) *youthful, young*

Я

^A **я** *(acc., gen.* меня́, *dat., the prepositional case* мне, *instr.* мной / мно́ю*) I*

^B **я́блоко** *(pl. nom.* я́блоки, *gen.* я́блок*) apple*

яви́ться *see* **явля́ться**

^C **явле́ние**

  1) *phenomenon*

  2) *scene (of a play)*

^A **явля́ться** / **яви́ться** (явлю́сь, я́вится, я́вятся)

  1) *appear*

  2) *(only ipf.)* (кем / чем) *be (smb. / smth.)*

^C **я́года** *berry*

^A **язы́к** *(E)*

  1) *tongue*

  2) *language*

^C **яйцо́** *(pl. nom.* я́йца, *gen.* яи́ц, *dat.* я́йцам*) egg*

  нести́ я́йца = *lay eggs*

  я́йца ку́рицу не у́чат = *don't teach your grandmother to suck eggs*

^A **янва́рь** *(gen.* января́*) January*

^A **я́ркий** (я́рок, ярка́, я́рко; я́рче)

  1) *bright*

  2) *gaudy, striking*

  3) *brilliant*

я́рче *see* **я́ркий**

^A **я́сный** (я́сен, ясна́, я́сно, я́сны́) *clear*

^A **я́щик**

  1) *box, chest*

  2) *drawer*